W9-BTH-186

EYE ON
Art

ANCIENT ROMAN ART AND ARCHITECTURE

by Don Nardo

LUCENT BOOKS
A part of Gale, Cengage Learning

GALE
CENGAGE Learning·

Detroit • New York • San Francisco • New Haven, Conn • Waterville, Maine • London

LIBRARY OF CONGRESS CATALOGING-IN-PUBLICATION DATA

Nardo, Don, 1947-
  Ancient Roman art and architecture / by Don Nardo.
    p. cm. -- (Eye on art)
  Summary: "These books provide a historical overview of the development of different types of art and artistic movements; explore the roots and influences of the genre; discuss the pioneers of the art and consider the changes the genre has undergone"-- Provided by publisher.
  Includes bibliographical references and index.
  ISBN 978-1-4205-0714-0 (hardback)
  1. Architecture, Roman--Juvenile literature. 2. Art, Roman--Juvenile literature. I. Title.
  NA310.N27 2012
  709.37--dc23
                                                           2011027227

Lucent Books
27500 Drake Rd
Farmington Hills MI 48331

ISBN-13: 978-1-4205-0714-0
ISBN-10: 1-4205-0714-1

Printed in the United States of America
1 2 3 4 5 6 7 15 14 13 12 11

CONTENTS

Foreword

"Art has no other purpose than to brush aside . . . everything that veils reality from us in order to bring us face to face with reality it-self."

—French philosopher Henri-Louis Bergson

Some thirty-one thousand years ago, early humans painted strikingly sophisticated images of horses, bison, rhinoceroses, bears, and other animals on the walls of a cave in southern France. The meaning of these elaborate pictures is unknown, although some experts speculate that they held ceremonial significance. Regardless of their intended purpose, the Chauvet-Pont-d'Arc cave paintings represent some of the first known expressions of the artistic impulse.

From the Paleolithic era to the present day, human beings have continued to create works of visual art. Artists have developed painting, drawing, sculpture, engraving, and many other techniques to produce visual representations of landscapes, the human form, religious and historical events, and countless other subjects. The artistic impulse also finds expression in glass, jewelry, and new forms inspired by new technology. Indeed, judging by humanity's prolific artistic output throughout history, one must conclude that the compulsion to produce art is an inherent aspect of being human, and the results are among humanity's greatest cultural achievements: masterpieces such as the architectural marvels of ancient Greece, Michelangelo's perfectly rendered statue *David*, Vincent van Gogh's visionary painting *Starry Night*, and endless other treasures.

The creative impulse serves many purposes for society. At its most basic level, art is a form of entertainment or the means for a satisfying or pleasant aesthetic experience. But art's true power lies not in its potential to entertain and delight but in its ability to enlighten, to reveal the truth, and by doing so to uplift the human spirit and transform the human race.

One of the primary functions of art has been to serve religion. For most of Western history, for example, artists were paid by the church to produce works with religious themes and subjects. Art was thus a tool to help human beings transcend mundane, secular reality and achieve spiritual enlightenment. One of the best-known, and largest-scale, examples of Christian religious art is the Sistine Chapel in the Vatican in Rome. In 1508 Pope Julius II commissioned Italian Renaissance artist Michelangelo to paint the chapel's vaulted ceiling, an area of 640 square yards (535 sq. m). Michelangelo spent four years on scaffolding, his neck craned, creating a panoramic fresco of some three hundred human figures. His paintings depict Old Testament prophets and heroes, sibyls of Greek mythology, and nine scenes from the Book of Genesis, including the Creation of Adam, the Fall of Adam and Eve from the Garden of Eden, and the Flood. The ceiling of the Sistine Chapel is considered one of the greatest works of Western art and has inspired the awe of countless Christian pilgrims and other religious seekers. As eighteenth-century German poet and author Johann Wolfgang von Goethe wrote, "Until you have seen this Sistine Chapel, you can have no adequate conception of what man is capable of."

In addition to inspiring religious fervor, art can serve as a force for social change. Artists are among the visionaries of any culture. As such, they often perceive injustice and wrongdoing and confront others by reflecting what they see in their work. One classic example of art as social commentary was created in May 1937, during the brutal Spanish civil war. On May 1 Spanish artist Pablo Picasso learned of the recent attack on the small Basque village of Guernica by German airplanes allied with fascist forces led by Francisco Franco. The German pilots had used the village for target practice, a three-hour bombing that killed sixteen hundred civilians. Picasso, living in Paris, channeled his outrage over the massacre into his painting *Guernica,* a black, white, and gray mural that depicts dismembered animals and fractured human figures whose faces are contorted in agonized expressions. Initially, critics and the public condemned the painting as an incoherent hodgepodge, but the work soon came to be seen as a powerful antiwar statement and remains an iconic symbol of the violence and terror that dominated world events during the remainder of the twentieth century.

The impulse to create art—whether painting animals with crude pigments on a cave wall, sculpting a human form from marble, or commemorating human tragedy in a mural—thus serves many purposes. It offers an entertaining diversion, nourishes the imagination and the spirit, decorates and beautifies the world, and chronicles the age. But underlying all these functions is the desire to reveal that which is obscure—to illuminate, clarify, and perhaps ennoble. As Picasso himself stated, "The purpose of art is washing the dust of daily life off our souls."

The Eye on Art series is intended to assist readers in understanding the various roles of art in society. Each volume offers an in-depth exploration of a major artistic movement, medium, figure, or profession. All books in the series are beautifully illustrated with full-color photographs and diagrams. Riveting narrative, clear technical explanation, informative sidebars, fully documented quotes, a bibliography, and a thorough index all provide excellent starting points for research and discussion. With these features, the Eye on Art series is a useful introduction to the world of art—a world that can offer both insight and inspiration.

Introduction

Practical Means for Practical Ends

When the western Roman Empire disintegrated in the fifth and sixth centuries, it was not strictly Roman civilization that disappeared. Culturally speaking it was Greco-Roman, a fusion of Roman and Greek ideas, customs, and arts. This was because many centuries before, the Romans had conquered the Greek lands clustered in the eastern Mediterranean sphere and in the process absorbed large portions of the Greek culture.

The two peoples had not started out on the same cultural paths by any means. Indeed, they initially had distinctly different national outlooks and spirits. This was well illustrated by their different views on what constituted art. The Greek way was to perceive beauty in nature and everyday life and to strive to find the truths that made nature tick and life worth living. Their art reflected the results of their search for such truths. It was, with a few notable exceptions, relatively small scale, economical, and to them meaningful and elegant in its simplicity.

The Roman Way

"But this was not the Roman way," the late noted classical scholar Edith Hamilton pointed out. When the Romans were rising from obscurity in west-central Italy in the 400s and 300s

B.C., she said, they "did not perceive beauty in everyday matters." Rather, in their eyes life "was a very serious and very arduous business," and they "had no time for what [they] would have thought of as a mere decoration of [their life]."[1]

Thus, the Greeks saw virtue in beauty and in the creative ways in which people tried to capture that beauty. In contrast, the early Romans had neither the time nor the interest in searching for beauty or for being creative. For the average early Roman, to be virtuous was to be serious, dignified, and self-disciplined, to work hard each day, and to show deep respect for the gods and one's community.

As the centuries wore on and Roman civilization grew and matured, its people did come to feel the need to express themselves and create something beautiful and lasting. But their approach proved quite different than that of the Greeks. With the exception of a few oversized statues and temples, the Greeks expressed their artistic feelings in simple ways and on a relatively smaller scale than the Romans. The Romans were great architects and builders, indeed by far the most impressive builders of ancient times. Their projects were nothing less than grandiose. "Roman genius was called into action by the enormous practical needs of a world empire," Hamilton said. So the true Roman artist was the engineer. He met his country's needs in superb fashion, by erecting

> buildings tremendous, indomitable, amphitheaters where eighty thousand could watch a spectacle, baths where three thousand could bathe at the same time, which nearly two thousand years have left practically intact. Bridges and aqueducts that spanned wide rivers and traversed great spaces with a beautiful, sure precision of soaring arches and massive piers. And always along with them the mighty Roman road, a monument of dogged, unconquerable human effort, huge stone jointed to huge stone, marching on and on irresistibly, through unknown hostile forests, over ramparts of mountains, across sun-baked deserts, to the very edges of the habitable world. That is the true art of Rome, the

This model of the City of Rome circa A.D. 100 shows the Romans' tradition of grand scale engineering and monumental architecture. The Colosseum is in the center and the Circus Maximus is in the lower left. One of Rome's aqueducts snakes between them through the city.

spontaneous expression of the Roman spirit, its keen realization of practical means to practical ends.[2]

University of London scholar Mortimer Wheeler agrees that building and architecture occupied the core of Roman art. "Roman art presumes Roman architecture," he wrote, "and at every turn spills over into it."[3]

Roman Individuality and Charm

Out of this remarkable artistic tradition of grand-scale engineering and monumental (large-scale) construction emerged the splendid Colosseum, where men, women, and wild animals fought one another to the death; Rome's main town square, the

Forum Romanum, lined with enormous government buildings; the truly stupendous Circus Maximus, a racetrack more than a third of a mile (0.5km) long; and tens of thousands of miles of paved roads from Britain to the Middle East.

However, despite the grandeur of these immense building projects, the Romans' smaller-scale arts should not be ignored. They produced large numbers of statues, portrait busts, and other sculptures; wall murals and other paintings; intricate mosaics; all manner of pottery, metalwork, and glassware; and countless coins bearing portraits of emperors and other leaders. In most cases Roman versions of these creative endeavors had little or no originality in their basic forms. Nevertheless, they possessed the stamp of Roman individuality and charm. The Romans did not invent portrait busts, for example. But unlike Greek versions, which tended to show idealized versions of people, most Roman ones depicted people as they were, wrinkles, scars, and all. That touch of distinct personality, that "Romanness," so to speak, infuses such arts with an innate quality that makes them eminently worth examining.

The other reason for studying Rome's smaller-scale art forms, the late historian Michael Grant said, was because they had so much influence on the arts of the modern Western world. "The art and architecture of the present day, our own work," he wrote, "would be far poorer had not its creators taken so much from the Romans. In other words, Roman art is not only good and interesting in itself, but is also the source of a great deal of our modern artistic production."[4] In that way the artistic spirit of the Romans, whose civilization vanished long ago, in a sense lives on today in peoples' lives and imaginations, quite often without their even suspecting it.

Greeks, Etruscans, and Romans

The Romans were in their own time, as well as in later ages, renowned for their construction of seemingly countless numbers of roads, bridges, amphitheaters, circuses, and other enormous structures. They did not invent most of these edifices, however. In fact, on the whole the Romans were not a very inventive people. Rather, from a cultural standpoint they were chronic borrowers, as the first-century-B.C. Roman historian Sallust readily admitted. "Whatever they found suitable among allies or foes," he said of his ancestors, "they put in practice at home with the greatest enthusiasm, preferring to imitate rather than envy the successful."[5]

In the disciplines of architecture and building, for example, the Romans borrowed the basic design of their temples primarily from the Greeks. Another important architectural borrowing was the arch, which over time became a Roman trademark. It was the Etruscans, a culturally advanced Italian folk whose cities were arrayed directly north of Rome, in the region called Etruria, who lent the Romans the arch. Indeed, of all the peoples from whom the Romans borrowed artistic ideas, the Greeks and Etruscans were in the forefront.

Architectural forms and many other cultural borrowings aside, though, the Romans were not just lazy, unthinking imitators. They were instead extremely ambitious, resourceful, and determined to succeed in every endeavor they pursued. They also had a remarkable talent for taking foreign concepts and combining them with their own native ideas. The results were buildings and other art forms that perfectly fulfilled their own personal, practical needs.

Moreover, the Roman versions of borrowed art forms tended to be bigger, or more numerous, or more durable, or all of these qualities, than the original versions. Thus, while the Greeks built temples mainly in Greece, the Romans erected Greek-like temples across all of Europe, North Africa, and much of the Middle East. Similarly, whereas the Etruscans used the arch in a few hundred buildings in northwest Italy, the Romans used that form in hundreds of thousands of structures across the known world.

The Roman temple of Zeus in Euromos dates from the second century A.D. and followed Greek temple design. The Romans built these temples throughout their empire.

Rome's cultural and artistic borrowing from foreign peoples took place over the course of many centuries. In fact, Roman civilization was extremely long-lived compared with most other ancient empires and societies. What is more, its development was complex, as over time it underwent several major political and social transformations. In turn, these affected the nature of Rome's artistic traditions and the artworks they produced. To better understand when and how the various trends in Roman art came about, a thumbnail sketch of Rome's chief historical periods is in order.

Major Eras of Roman Civilization

Ancient Roman civilization existed for at least fifteen centuries. Modern experts have found evidence of small villages on one or more of Rome's famous seven hills (in west-central Italy) as early as 1000 B.C. The Romans themselves recognized a traditional founding date of 753 B.C. There might well be some truth in this tradition, as it may represent a faint historical memory of the unification of those early villages into a central town called Rome.

Historians divide Rome's long life as a national entity (a country, empire, or other political unit) into several general time periods. The name of each period also defines the kind of government in use in that era. Thus, the first period—called the Monarchy, lasting from about 753 to 509 B.C.—was the era in which kings ruled Rome. Both before and during the Monarchy's early years, the Romans produced little or nothing that would today be defined as art. They were initially a conservative, austere, and culturally backward agricultural people who lived in simple huts made of dried mud and thatch and disdained luxuries of any kind.

However, the Romans could not long ignore their northern neighbors, the Etruscans. It was clear that the cities of Etruria were considerably more culturally advanced than Rome, and this impressed the Romans. So they began borrowing ideas, particularly political, religious, and architectural

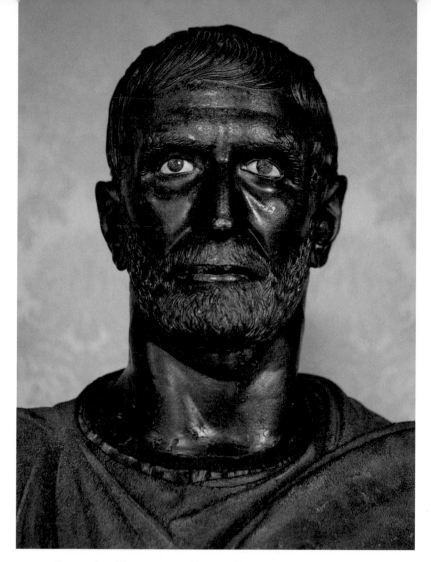

This Republican Roman bronze bust from the third century B.C., known as Capitoline Brutus, shows the influence of Etruscan and Greek styles.

ones, from the Etruscans. Some Etruscans actually moved to Rome. A handful of them rose to challenge the authority of the leading Roman landowners—the patricians, who formed an emerging local nobility—and became kings of that still small and backward city-state.

The end of the Monarchy came in 509 B.C. when the patricians tossed out their reigning king, ended the kingship itself, and founded the Roman Republic (509–30 B.C.). This new, more enlightened government had the Senate, a legislature made up solely of patricians; two elected administrator-generals, called consuls, who served jointly for a year; and other elected officials.

Under the Republic's banners, Rome began to expand outward from central Italy and one by one conquered its neighbors. This included the Etruscans in the north, the Samnites in the hills of central Italy, and the Greek city-states that had recently grown up across southern Italy. These and other peoples the Romans overran had cultural and artistic ideas and traditions that the Romans admired, envied, and therefore readily absorbed. They became especially enamored of Greek culture, and in the 200s B.C. Greek arts filtered into and steadily reshaped Roman society. This process continued as the Romans defeated both the large maritime empire of Carthage in the western Mediterranean and the Greek city-states and kingdoms in the eastern reaches of that sea.

By the beginning of the first century B.C., Rome had created an enormous realm consisting of nearly all the lands bordering that wide waterway. "The entire Mediterranean Sea was a Roman lake," historian Naphtali Lewis remarks, "and those who lived on and around it looked to Rome as the [decider] of their fortunes."[6] But ominous cracks soon began to form in the republican government's edifice. Later in the first century a series of destructive civil wars brought the Republic to its knees, and the victor of the final conflict, Octavian, managed to acquire a wide range of powers. The Senate, by now an impotent body, bestowed on him the name of Augustus, the "revered one." His ascendancy as an absolute dictator (later called an emperor) marked the beginning of a new Roman era and government—the Roman Empire (30 B.C.–A.D. 476).

The early Empire witnessed a golden age of Roman literature, as well as a maturing phase of sculpture, architecture, and several other art forms that Rome had originally borrowed from others. Roman temples, amphitheaters, government buildings, and other structures were erected across the realm. Also, government officials and private citizens alike commissioned Greek and Roman artists to create statues, wall paintings, and mosaic floors to adorn Roman towns and homes.

The arts thrived until they had to be temporarily neglected during the so-called Anarchy, a period of civil strife and foreign

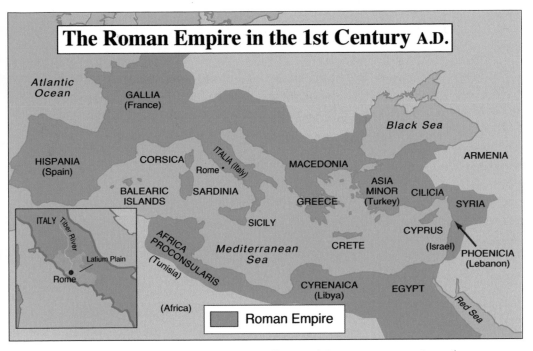

The Roman Empire in the 1st Century A.D.

Atlantic Ocean

GALLIA (France)

Black Sea

HISPANIA (Spain)

CORSICA

ITALIA (Italy)

Rome

MACEDONIA

ARMENIA

BALEARIC ISLANDS

SARDINIA

ASIA MINOR (Turkey)

CILICIA

GREECE

SYRIA

SICILY

CYPRUS

ITALY

Tiber River

AFRICA PROCONSULARIS (Tunisia)

Mediterranean Sea

CRETE

(Israel)

PHOENICIA (Lebanon)

Latium Plain

Rome

CYRENAICA (Libya)

EGYPT

Red Sea

(Africa)

Roman Empire

invasions in the mid-200s A.D. But architecture, portrait sculptures, and other arts revived in Rome's final national era, which modern scholars sometimes call the Later Empire (A.D. 284–476). Toward the end of that period, Roman architecture displayed new and distinct forms under the influence of the Christians, who came to power in the mid-300s. Many former pagan (non-Christian) structures had already been transformed into Christian churches by the time the last western Roman emperor was deposed from his throne in A.D. 476.

"A Curious Love-Hate Affair"

During most of these broad, eventful time periods, Roman arts remained highly dependent on Greek arts. In large part this was because the Romans long recognized that Greek art and several other Greek cultural ideas and values were superior to their own. As Michael Grant explained:

> The relationship of the Romans to the Greeks was a curious love-hate affair. Of course, we cannot tell what the ordinary [Roman] felt about the Greeks, but we can guess that he or she did not estimate them very

highly. After all, Rome had conquered them. . . . [The Romans] thought (rightly) that Greek law was nothing like as good as Roman, and they regarded the [Greek] city-states as small-scale and parochial [narrow-minded]. But on the other hand, an unbound admiration was felt [by the Romans] for the Greek past, with all its literary and artistic traditions. [In fact] the debt of Rome to Greece was unimaginably enormous. Rome, and Roman architecture and art, could never have existed at all if it had not been for the Greeks before them.[7]

ROME TAKEN CAPTIVE

The late Columbia University scholar Moses Hadas commented on how one of the Romans' greatest achievements was to absorb numerous aspects of Greek art and culture and make them their own. This ensured that when various facets of Roman culture passed on to medieval Europe after Rome's fall, some aspects of Greek culture passed on, too. Hadas wrote:

Rome's career spanned a millennium. In that time Rome assembled the greatest empire the world had seen. But the size and stability of [that realm] are not the sum of Rome's claim to greatness. A more enduring claim lies in Rome's marked genius in nourishing and embellishing the intellectual and cultural achievements of the Greek world that it [had] conquered, and spreading them across Europe. Roman architecture, art, literature, and religion—all showing the influence of Greece, bear the unmistakable stamp of Roman power and assurance. Nevertheless, [the noted Roman poet] Horace's statement is true: "Captive Greece took Rome captive."

Moses Hadas. *Imperial Rome.* New York: Time-Life, 2001, p. 11.

The Romans did not realize, of course, that as they consistently absorbed and subtly reshaped Greek architecture and other arts, they were slowly but surely merging the two civilizations into one. A true Greco-Roman cultural fusion, it would centuries later become known as "classical civilization." That momentous merger assured that Greek arts and ideas would, along with Roman ones, survive the Roman Empire's demise and go on to influence later generations of Westerners. As Mortimer Wheeler says, "Roman art in its broadest sense was enlarging and at the same time almost utterly transforming the Greek tradition, preparing [for] that astonishing afterlife in which it was to dominate the post-Renaissance world down to the noonday of modern times."[8]

It must be emphasized that the Greeks did not powerfully reshape Roman culture, including its arts, overnight. Rather, this happened over the course of several centuries in what can be seen as succeeding waves of cultural influences. The first major wave was indirect. This was because Greek culture initially exerted profound effects on Etruscan culture, which later had similar influences on Roman society.

Greece and Etruria

The Etruscans first encountered Greek culture and arts circa 760 B.C. In that year a Greek trading post was established on the small island of Ischia, lying near the northern rim of the Bay of Naples in western Italy. "This settlement," noted Ithaca College scholar Nancy H. Ramage writes, "marked the beginning of a long and mutually profitable exchange between the Greeks and [Italian] peoples. Greek pottery . . . served as models for the Italic potters, who imitated them in their local clays. . . . The Etruscans absorbed these influences from Greece [and] incorporated them into their own art and culture."[9]

In the following seventy years or so, numerous other Greek settlements appeared on the coasts of southern Italy and the nearby island of Sicily. In addition to showing the Etruscans new pottery techniques, some Greeks settled and worked in Etruscan towns. They, along with Greek traders, inspired the

This Etruscan black dipper cup from 700–675 B.C. shows the influence on Etruscan art of the Greek colonies in southern Italy.

Etruscans to absorb Greek artistic motifs (styles), fabric designs, and clothing styles. The Etruscans borrowed the Greeks' alphabet and became literate. In addition, Greek traders brought luxury goods and artworks from the eastern Mediterranean to Italy, among them carved ivory items from Syria and silver cups and bowls from Cyprus. This inflow of foreign artworks motivated Etruscan artisans to create versions of their own, including copies of the more popular Greek items. For instance, pottery from Corinth, in southern Greece, became especially popular in Etruria.

The Etruscans also adopted Greek temple architecture. Before contact with the Greeks, the Etruscans had no temples and performed their rituals at altars set up in fields or town squares. In time, however, city-states across Etruria began building temples similar to those of the Greeks. There were some differences, to be sure. For example, early Etruscan temples had fewer columns than Greek ones and featured small wings on the sides. Still, these structures were clearly based on Greek models.

This steady transformation of Etruscan society, architecture, and arts caused by contact with Greek culture continued apace. In the 600s and early 500s B.C., a group of Etruscan city-states expanded in size and power and extended their influence across large parts of Italy and even beyond. In the words of historians Graeme Barker and Tom Rasmussen, Etruscan culture emerged "as one of the leading lights on the Mediterranean stage."[10]

Rome and Etruria

During this period of Etruscan expansion, the Roman city-state, then in the middle of its Monarchy period, was still very small and culturally backward. The urban center on the seven hills, along with the outer villages and farms under its control, covered no more than 600 square miles (1,555 sq. km), roughly the size of New York City. Modern experts estimate that the total population of Roman territory, including slaves, was then about 260,000.

Etruria's territory and population at that time, though difficult to estimate, was certainly a good deal bigger than Rome's. Also, the Etruscans were, thanks to the Greeks, far more culturally advanced than the Romans. It is hardly surprising, therefore, that the Romans adopted a number of customs and ideas, including some key architectural ones, from their northern neighbors.

After visiting Etruscan cities, Roman leaders became painfully aware that their own little town was practically a ramshackle slum in comparison. The Etruscans had installed sewer drains, for instance, while the Romans still dumped their household wastes in backyards or even into the streets. Etruria also boasted a number of large stone buildings and bridges. Not to be outdone, Rome's rulers called for importing Etruscan stonemasons and builders, who taught the Romans their methods (many of which had come from Greek builders). During this phase of Roman-Etruscan relations, one of the more useful and distinctive borrowings from Etruria was the arch, which the Romans were destined to make their own and employ on a vast scale.

The Romans also borrowed some of the gods the Etruscans worshipped. In turn, these deities' forms, personalities, and functions had earlier been strongly influenced by Greek models. A prominent example was the god Jupiter, leader of the Roman pantheon (group of gods), who was adopted from the Etruscan deity Tinia. Before contact with the Greeks, the Etruscans had viewed him, like their other gods, as a vague, formless spirit dwelling somewhere in nature. Under Greek religious influences, however, Tinia took on human form as the equivalent of Zeus, leader of the Greek Olympian gods. So when the Romans borrowed the Etruscan Tinia and made him Jupiter, they were indirectly adopting the Greek Zeus. Among the other Etruscan-Greek gods the Romans adopted were Jupiter's divine wife, Juno (from the Etruscan Uni and the Greek Hera), patron goddess of women, and Minerva (from the Etruscan Menerva and the Greek Athena), the goddess of war and wisdom, who also protected craftspeople.

AN ETRUSCAN TEMPLE DESCRIBED

*The first-century-*B.C.* Roman architect Vitruvius saw many Etruscan temples firsthand and gave a detailed description of their proper layout. It reads in part:*

The place where the temple is to be built, having been divided on its length into six parts, deduct one and let the rest be given to its width. Then let the length be divided into two equal parts, of which let the inner be reserved as space for the *cellae* [inner chambers], and the part next to the front left for the arrangement of the columns. Next let the width be divided into ten parts. Of these, let three on the right and three on the left be given to the smaller *cella* . . . and the other four devoted to the middle of the temple. Let the space in front of the *cellae*, in the pronaos [front porch], be marked out for columns.

Vitruvius. *On Architecture.* Translated by Morris H. Morgan. Cambridge, MA: Harvard University Press, 1914, p. 122.

This replica of the Etruscan Temple of Aletrium is located in the Villa Giulia Museum in Rome.

The Second and Third Waves

With these and other borrowings from the Etruscans, the first, indirect wave of Greek cultural influence on Rome was complete. The second wave occurred during the early to mid-200s B.C., when the Romans' territorial expansion brought them

Traces of Greek influence can be seen on the second-century-B.C. Temple of Fortuna Virilis in Rome. The columns are topped with Ionic capitals.

face to face with the Greek cities of southern Italy. Some of the Greek cities were larger than Rome, and all were more culturally and artistically advanced.

Between 275 and 265 B.C., the Romans conquered these cities, although they did so strictly from a military and political standpoint. From a cultural and artistic perspective, it was the Italian Greeks who conquered the Romans. Direct Greek influences on Rome proved stronger than the earlier ones, which had been filtered through Etruscan civilization. As the late historian William G. Sinnigen put it:

> The presence of Greek towns in Italy gave a tremendous stimulus to the cultural development of the Italians. The more highly developed Greek . . . political institutions, Greek art, Greek literature, and Greek mythology found a ready reception among the Italian peoples and profoundly affected their political and intellectual progress. Traces of this Greek influence are nowhere more noticeable than in the case of Rome itself, and the cultural ascendancy which Greece thus early established over Rome was destined to last until the breakup of the Roman Empire.[11]

Perhaps the most visually obvious of these "traces" of Greek influence were the basics of Greek temple architecture, which the Romans incorporated into their own temples, as the Etruscans had before them. The main structural elements of this distinctly Greek architectural form were a rectangular structure with front and back porches; triangular gables, called pediments, situated above the porches and beneath the slanting roof eaves; and a pteron (TAIR-on), a row of columns stretching all the way around the inner structure and supporting the roof. Greek temples were erected in three major styles, called orders, each based on the look of its columns. Doric temples had columns with plain slabs in their capitals, or tops. Ionic capitals featured curved scrolls called volutes, and Corinthian capitals had ornate masses of masonry acanthus leaves. The Romans particularly liked Corinthian columns (perhaps because they saw in them an air of imperial splendor) and used them far more than the Greeks did.

Still more admiration for Greek arts resulted from the third wave of Greek influences on Rome. This development occurred in the wake of Rome's large-scale conquest of the Greek lands in the eastern Mediterranean in the second century B.C. By no means were all Romans suddenly seized with the desire to have or to copy Greek artworks. In fact, many Romans, especially lower-class and uneducated ones, remained culturally backward. (After a Roman army sacked the Greek city of Corinth in 146 B.C., the second-century Greek historian Polybius personally witnessed Roman soldiers carrying artworks they had looted. Among them was a painting that they threw to the ground and used as a surface on which to play dice.)

As time went on, however, more and more middle- and upper-class Romans became fascinated with Greek culture and could not resist its many allures. They also recognized that embracing Greek culture and its arts enhanced their image in the world at large. According to noted historian of ancient art Paul Zanker, large numbers of envious and ambitious Romans wanted "to acquire the splendid culture of the [Greek-influenced] Mediterranean world in order that they might take part in international diplomacy as equals." In the century or so that followed, this steadily and fundamentally changed Roman society. "The adoption of certain features of Greek elite lifestyle, such as clothing, dining rituals, and forms of relaxation and leisure, but also Greek philosophy, poetry, and art, led to a new system of values and a new self-image within the Roman upper class. . . . This process also involved changes in the functions of—and the demand for—artworks."[12]

A Wonder to Behold

Once the architectural, sculptural, and other artistic floodgates had opened for the Romans, most notably during the first century and a half of the Empire, there was no stopping the march of Roman art and architecture. In size, audacity, and sheer numbers, production of all manner of artworks across the

realm far exceeded that of Greece, and for that matter all other ancient societies. In the words of Boston University scholar Fred S. Kleiner, the Roman capital became "a wonder to behold, crammed with [architecturally magnificent] shrines to the pantheon of Roman gods; theaters, amphitheaters, and baths to entertain the masses; [imposing] forums for the conduct of public business; [and] triumphal arches to advertise the emperors' achievements. . . . The city awed all who saw it for the first time, whether rich or poor, citizen or foreigner."[13] In this way, incredibly, a city that had once featured dirt streets, primitive huts, and virtually no artistic output eventually grew into a shining showcase of arts for the ages.

A reconstruction of the Forum Romanum, which was the political and economic center of Rome.

2

Amphitheaters and Other Giant Structures

I n the late Republic and early Empire, the Romans seized control of large portions of Europe, North Africa, and the Middle East. In the process they fashioned one of the largest and most diverse territorial realms in human history. For those in Rome's elite circles, it was no longer acceptable for their capital and other major cities to be cluttered, dirty, and unimposing. There was a growing feeling that a grand empire must have an equally grand capital that would impress all who visited it. In Edith Hamilton's words:

> As Rome grew rich and strong and proud, she felt, of course, the need to display her power by a visible magnificence, and she built splendid temples and palaces and triumphal arches. . . . To the Roman, the big was in itself admirable. The biggest temple in the world was as such better than the rest. If a Corinthian capital was lovely, two, one on top of the other, would be twice as lovely.[14]

Following this reasoning, architects, engineers, and builders—long the most characteristic and distinguished of Rome's artists—raised thousands of monumental structures. Among them were amphitheaters like the Colosseum, where gladiators' bouts and other public games took place; circuses in which chariot races were staged; theaters for play production; gigantic bathhouses that contained gymnasiums and shopping malls as well as bathing facilities; palaces to house the imperial families; and many others. In size and number, many of these enormous edifices totally surpassed those of the Greeks, Egyptians, Carthaginians, Babylonians, and other peoples who lived on the periphery of the Mediterranean Sea.

Just as important as the size and number of these structures was *how* they were built. Many of the construction methods and materials the Romans developed (some of them borrowed from the Greeks and Etruscans) survived the fall of the western Empire in the late 400s. Later builders adopted them, which made the creation of large-scale structures in medieval and early modern times possible. As one modern observer puts it: "All the architecture of the Middle Ages and more recent times, right up to the introduction of iron into building structures and thus almost to our own day, depends on the Roman construction techniques of the arch and vault, bricks and concrete."[15]

"When Falls the Colosseum"

Of all the giant architectural forms the Romans erected on a regular basis, none came to symbolize the unique combination of Rome's power and artistic achievement more than the amphitheater. The ruins of Roman amphitheaters still stand at intervals across Europe and North Africa. Although all were clearly impressive structures in their heyday, the most imposing and inspiring of all was the Colosseum in Rome. As the building began to crumble in the post-Roman world, it came to have romantic, mythic, and even heroic qualities. More than any other single structure in the Western world, it still represents that special brand of monumental art that was distinctly Roman.

The medieval English churchman and historian widely known as the Venerable Bede sensed this special quality inhabiting Roman amphitheaters, especially the mighty Colosseum. He believed that massive oval stone arena was a timeless symbol of the so-called eternal city of Rome, which was still very

The Colosseum in Rome. Built in the first century A.D., it has become the symbol of the Romans' brand of monumental art and architecture.

much standing in his day. This was what moved him to pen the now famous words, "While stands the Colosseum, Rome shall stand. When falls the Colosseum, Rome [the city itself] shall fall. And when Rome falls—the world."[16]

Bede and other people of the Middle Ages had no inkling of how the Colosseum and other Roman amphitheaters came to be. How they evolved, how they were designed and built, and exactly how they were used had become mysteries in the wake of Roman civilization's demise. In modern times archaeologists managed to solve those mysteries. A brief examination of the development and construction of these remarkable monuments reveals the major goals, materials, and building techniques the Romans employed for most of their giant structures.

Early Amphitheaters

The men who designed the Colosseum in the first century A.D. did not invent its special architectural form and features. Rather, the building was the end product and pinnacle of a long evolution of architectural concepts used in smaller, simpler, and less durable structures. These originally developed as places to stage fights between gladiators.

The Romans initially borrowed the custom of such fights from Etruscan funerals, in which two men, usually prisoners of war, fought near a dead person's grave. It was believed that the blood spilled in the combat would ensure that the spirit of the deceased individual would make it to the afterlife. These funeral fights caught on in upper-class Roman circles in the late 300s and early 200s B.C. and first took place in the capital city in 264 B.C. Over time, such ritual battles grew into a kind of public spectacle the Romans called a *munus* (plural: *munera*).

For a long time the *munera* were staged outside, most often in town squares (forums) or marketplaces. But as the number of spectators steadily grew, the Romans erected arenas with wooden seats in which the audience could sit and watch for several hours. It appears that these early arenas were portable. Gangs of carpenters assembled them in a marketplace, forum, or other place and dismantled them when the bouts were over.

Eventually, larger, more elaborate wooden arenas having seats for thousands of people were built. They probably remained in place for two, three, or more years before making way for new temples, housing, or other structures. It is likely that at least some of these first wooden amphitheaters were erected by reliable architects and builders. But as has been true in all ages, sometimes less-skilled and less-reputable building contractors used substandard materials and slipshod methods. That this occasionally led to tragedy is known because the first-century Roman historian Tacitus described the collapse of a wooden amphitheater in a town north of Rome in A.D. 27. The architect, he said,

> neither rested its foundations on solid ground nor fastened the wooden superstructure securely. He had undertaken the project not because of great wealth or municipal ambition but for sordid profits. . . . The packed structure collapsed, subsiding both inwards and outwards and [overwhelmed] a huge crowd of spectators and bystanders. Those killed at the outset of the catastrophe at least escaped torture. . . . More pitiable were those, mangled but not yet dead, who knew their wives and children lay there too. . . . Fifty thousand people were mutilated or crushed in the disaster.[17]

The Pompeian Amphitheater

Such catastrophes constituted at least one reason that Roman builders turned to using stone for these and other large public structures. Clearly, a stone amphitheater was not only stronger and safer, but also more permanent. The first all-stone amphitheater built in Italy appeared in 80 B.C., about two decades before the Roman world plunged into the series of civil wars that eventually brought down the Republic. The structure was located in the large town of Pompeii (having a population of roughly twenty thousand), on the Bay of Naples.

In later ages Pompeii became famous for its sudden demise and burial in the eruption of the volcano Mount Vesuvius in A.D. 79. Though this was an awful calamity for the inhabitants, it turned out to be a stroke of good fortune for modern excavators and historians. The volcanic ash that rained down on and entombed the town ended up protecting and preserving many of its buildings.

That included the amphitheater, which survives today in near-perfect condition. Like the more ruined Roman amphitheaters that endure elsewhere in Europe, the Pompeian version is oval in shape. It measures 445 by 341 feet (136m by 104m) and in its glory accommodated about twenty thousand people. They sat on stone seats that rose in tiers supported on the bottom and at the back by large earthen embankments.

The architect who devised this clever and very sturdy arrangement is unknown. (Very few names of Roman architects and other artists are known today.) However, the names of the two Pompeian magistrates who sponsored the building —Gaius Quinctius Valgus and Marcius Porcius—did survive. This is because the ash from the eruption kept the inscription they carved to dedicate the building intact. (The ash also preserved an ad on a nearby city wall that reads, "The gladiatorial troop hired by Aulus Suettius Certus will fight in Pompeii on May 31. There will also be a wild animal hunt.")[18]

The first all-stone amphitheater built in Italy was constructed in Pompeii in 80 B.C.

Constructing the Colosseum

Other full-size stone amphitheaters like the one in Pompeii began to sprout up across the Empire in the first century A.D., during the reigns of some of the early emperors. Eventually, these structures numbered more than seventy-five. Most were more sophisticated and difficult to erect than the Pompeian version, mainly because they did not rely on masses of earth to support the walls and seating tiers. Instead, these extremely heavy elements rested on an intricate system of stone piers (upright supports), arches, and other architectural components.

The most impressive of all these buildings—the Colosseum—was also the first large, permanent one in the imperial capital. Its original name was the *Amphitheatrum Flavium*, or

This cut-away reconstruction of the Colosseum shows the five levels of the amphitheater built by the Flavians.

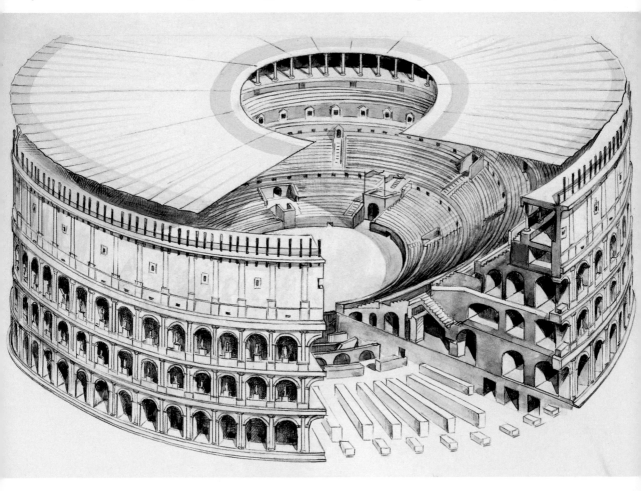

"Amphitheater of the Flavians." This was a reference to the noble Flavian family, which produced the three emperors who made the structure possible. They were Vespasian (reigned 69–79), who initiated it, and his sons Titus (79–81) and Domitian (81–96), who finished its construction. (The name *Colosseum* did not come into general use until medieval times.)

The first step taken by Vespasian's builders, as was the case in all large-scale Roman buildings, was to create a proper foundation. It had to be strong enough to support the millions of tons of stone, wood, dirt, and people that would eventually press down on it. Almost without exception, the material the Romans used for such foundations was concrete.

Long before, the Greeks had employed a mixture of lime, sand, and water to make a hard-drying mortar, and Roman builders had adopted this idea. But as they usually did, the practical, resourceful Romans soon improved on it. In the third century B.C., they found a much stronger material, which they made by adding what they thought was a special kind of sand to lime, in a ratio of two or three to one. (Discovered near Mount Vesuvius, it was not actually sand, but rather a kind of volcanic ash that had formed in eruptions thousands of years before.) The foundation for an amphitheater, especially one the size of the Colosseum, required several layers of concrete. Each had to dry thoroughly before the next one could be added.

Once this tedious but essential process had been completed, the workers began placing the first level of vertical stone piers atop the massive foundation. These supported a second level, or story, with its own set of piers, and so forth. The structure had four major levels. The first was a bit more than 34 feet (10m) high; the second stood 38 feet (11m) tall; the third was also 38 feet high; and the fourth was more than 45 feet (14m) tall. That made the total height of the building about 156 feet (47.5m), about equivalent to that of a modern fifteen-story building.

With few exceptions, the piers on each level were joined together by graceful stone arches. Each arch was composed of two arcs (curved lines) of wedge-shaped stones, called voussoirs (voo-SWARS), which met each other at the top in a central piece, the keystone. Each level had hundreds of archways. It also featured many straight barrel vaults, walled corridors topped by rounded ceilings. These fanned away from the central section toward the building's outer perimeter in a radial fashion, like the spokes of a wheel. Along the way, they intersected with several long, curving corridors, also in the shape of barrel vaults, that encircled the structure's outer sections. The piers supporting the innermost of these concentric corridors "supported the two chief zones of seats," scholar D.S. Robertson explains. Following the brilliant design of the architect (whose identity remains unknown), "the heavy marble seating was entirely supported by these radiating walls. These walls were interrupted on the ground level by two more concentric vaulted corridors near the [central] arena, and the spaces between them were utilized for staircases and passages, all vaulted."[19]

To reach the upper levels, the workers used scaffolding quite similar to the kind employed by modern carpenters, plasterers, and painters. Also, to lift heavy stones and other building materials to the upper levels, Roman workers used various hoists, including large cranes. One of the strongest and most ingenious had a circular cage, or drum, containing a treadmill that several workers operated by walking on it. Part of the drum's support structure, the first-century-B.C. Roman architect Vitruvius said, consisted of a tall wooden block, or support, surrounded by an elaborate system of ropes and pulleys. These "are carried right and left of the drum on the axle," he wrote, "and are tied so as to hold there. Then another rope is wound round the drum . . . and the drum, being trodden by men, can produce [quick] results."[20] A sculpted relief of this very machine, with five men (possibly slaves) operating the treadmill, was discovered in a tomb near Rome in 1848. Archaeologists have dated the carving to roughly A.D. 100, shortly after the Colosseum was completed.

Upon that completion, the great amphitheater measured 620 by 513 feet (189m by 156m). The oval arena floor was 287 feet (87m) long by 180 feet (55m) wide. The building's seats

LIKE SOME AWFUL DREAM

Monumental Roman buildings were made to last, and substantial portions of many still exist. Of these, the Colosseum is among the most impressive, as captured in this atmospheric description of its hulking ruin in 1832 by popular American landscape painter Thomas Cole.

The Colosseum [is] stupendous, yet beautiful in its destruction, [and] he who would see and feel [its] grandeur . . . must spend his hour there, at night, when the moon is shedding over it its magic splendor. Let him ascend to its higher terraces, at that pensive time, and gaze down into the abyss, or hang his eye upon the ruinous ridge, where it gleams in the moon-rays, and charges boldly against the deep blue heaven. The mighty spectacle, mysterious and dark, opens beneath the eye more like some awful dream than an earthly reality, a vision of the valley and shadow of death, rather than the substantial work of man. Could man, indeed, have ministered either to its erection or its ruin? . . . It was once a crater of human passions . . . but now all is still desolation. In the morning the warbling of birds makes the quiet air melodious; in the hushed and holy twilight, the low chanting of monkish solemnities soothes the startled ear.

Quoted in Louis L. Noble. *The Life and Works of Thomas Cole*. New York: Sheldon, Blakeman, 1856, pp. 159–160.

no longer exist, so it is difficult to tell how many people it originally held. But the general consensus of modern experts is that the seating capacity was roughly fifty thousand. The outer decorations included pilasters (half columns set partway into the walls) in the Doric, Ionic, and Corinthian orders, and statues of people and animals.

Circuses and Theaters

Other large-scale Roman buildings employed the basic architectural forms, materials, and techniques that went into the Colosseum and other amphitheaters. They included the arch, vault, barrel vault, and the three Greek architectural orders (especially the Corinthian); marble, travertine (a finally textured type of limestone), tufa (a lightweight volcanic stone), bricks (both sun dried and baked), and concrete; hammers and metal chisels to trim and shape the stones; the *chorobates*, a wooden device shaped like a bench that indicated when a foundation or other horizontal layer was level; scaffolding; and various mechanical hoists for lifting heavy materials.

The Romans loved chariot racing and the Circus Maximus in Rome allowed over 150,000 spectators to watch the races.

These and a few other simple tools and materials were all that Roman architects and builders needed to create a type of public games facility that dwarfed even the Colosseum. Known as a circus, it was a long stadium-like structure in which the

Rome's Most Famous Architect

M arcus Vitruvius Pollio, then and now called Vitruvius for short, was one of the few Roman architects and other artists whose name was not lost over the centuries. The main reason for this is that he published a book on architecture and the arts (titled *On Architecture*) that was widely distributed in the early Empire and has survived complete. The dates of his birth and death are unknown. But some evidence suggests that he was active as an architect from roughly 46 to 30 B.C. Apparently, he wrote his book in the 20s B.C., after he had retired. In the preface of the work, which is in ten parts then called "books," he told the first emperor, Augustus, "In the following books, I have expounded a complete system of architecture." True to his word, Vitruvius proceeded to describe nearly every existing form of Greek and Roman architecture, along with common building materials, town planning, civil engineering, water systems, painting and other forms of decoration, and the various mechanical devices of his time. After the collapse of western Rome, his book lived on, and the edition published in 1486 became a sudden best seller among European architects. The building style they founded dominated Europe for centuries and is occasionally still used today.

Vitruvius. *On Architecture*. Vol. 1. Translated by Frank Granger. Cambridge, MA: Harvard University Press, 2002, p. 5.

Romans' favorite sport—chariot racing—took place. The Greeks held horse and chariot races in flat, open areas called hippodromes. The spectators stood along the sides or sat on earthen embankments that had been piled up nearby. The Romans initially used Greek-style hippodromes, too. But over time, they added wooden, and later stone, bleachers along the sides, along with other improvements.

The Theater of Marcellus was opened around 11 B.C. and could hold fourteen thousand theater goers.

The biggest and most famous Roman circus, the Circus Maximus, in Rome, underwent such continuous upgrades beginning in about 600 B.C., during the Monarchy. Starting gates for the horses were installed in 329 B.C., for example. Additions were also made to the *euripus* (or *spina*), the long, spine-like barrier running down the middle of the track, around which the chariots raced. As archaeologist Lesley Adkins points out, it became "lavishly ornamented with sculptures, obelisks, water basins, and fountains."[21] These and other decorations made the building a kind of giant artwork in and of itself. Here, *giant* is the operative word. The Great Circus, as many ancients called it, was 2,040 feet (622m) long and 450 feet (137m) wide. The seating capacity was at least 150,000, and another 100,000 fans may have watched the races from the hills overlooking the facility.

As was the case with circuses and amphitheaters, Roman theaters designed to present stage shows began as makeshift wooden structures. Over time, they grew more permanent, increasingly elaborate, and more highly decorated. One early wooden theater mentioned in ancient sources sat up to eighty thousand people and featured numerous statues and colorful tapestries.

In 55 B.C., near the end of the Republic, the first stone theater rose in Rome. Called the Theater of Pompey, it was shaped like half of a pie and had rising tiers of seats along the inside of the curved wall. On the inside of the straight wall, behind the stage, loomed a large masonry wall, the *scaenae frons*, which was magnificently decorated with statues, paintings, gold-leafed Corinthian pillars, and other luxuries. "In front of the stage," Adkins says, "was a trough or trench for the curtain, which was lowered into the trough [thereby revealing the stage] at the beginning of the performance and raised at the end. There were also smaller curtains to screen off parts of the *scaenae frons* as required."[22]

The Theater of Pompey accommodated about eight thousand people. An even bigger facility for plays—the Theater of Marcellus, inaugurated in the capital in 11 B.C.—sat fourteen thousand people. In all, the Roman Empire eventually had nearly 130 such theaters.

Bathhouses and Basilicas

If the number of Roman theaters sounds large, consider that Rome's communal bathhouses, some of which were enormous, were built by the thousands. During the early Republic, these structures were small and privately run. Sometimes the owner rented the building to another person, who ran it on a daily basis. One such arrangement was revealed in some graffiti found on a wall in Pompeii. The graffiti read in part, "On the estate of Julia Felix, the daughter of Spurius Felix, the following are for rent: an elegant bath suitable for the best people, shops, rooms above them, and second story apartments."[23]

These modest-sized structures had tiny bathing facilities by later standards. Typically they consisted of a few terra-cotta (baked clay) bathtubs and sometimes one or two small pools recessed into the floor.

In the late Republic and early Empire, however, large-scale public bathhouses outfitted with complex bathing equipment swiftly spread across the Roman world. The largest, built and run by the government, featured numerous interconnected rooms with hot and cold pools, saunas, swimming pools, exercise areas, handball courts, reading rooms, snack bars, and shops. These immense, palace-like buildings were also decorated with splendid artworks, including larger-than-life-size statues, paintings, and mosaics. An outstanding example was the Baths of Caracalla, erected in the early 200s A.D. It measured 1,107 by 1,104 feet (337m by 336m). No less impressive, its roof rested on 252 columns, 16 of which were 5 feet (1.5m) across and more than 40 feet (12m) tall.

Another large Roman public building with a massive inner space and very high ceiling was the basilica, which began to develop in the late third century B.C. It was a "heavily decorated meeting place or public center used for various purposes," researcher Matthew Bunson writes. "Basilicas served most often to house the meetings of governmental groups or commissions."[24] Although basilica designs varied somewhat from place to place, the average version featured an enormous open central space, the nave, with aisles running parallel to it on its sides. It also had a semicircular chamber called an apse on one or both ends.

One of the most impressive basilicas in Rome was the Basilica of Maxentius (later renamed the Basilica of Constantine), large parts of which survive. "This was one of the architectural marvels of the Roman world," Michael Grant states. "Its plan eclipses all earlier basilicas in grandeur and brilliance. The interior must have seemed to soar upwards without weight, for every wall-space [contained] windows or niches, [making it look] open to the sky."[25]

In the Later Empire, as the Christians rose to power in the imperial government, the basilica was adopted as the standard

After visiting a large Roman bathhouse, the second-century-A.D. Greek author Lucian of Samosata wrote about some of its many attractive features, saying in part:

The building [is very well lit, and] the entrance is high, with a flight of broad steps [that are] easy to ascend. On entering, one is received into a public hall of good size with ample accommodations for servants and attendants. On the left are the lounging rooms, also of just the right sort for a bath, attractive, brightly lighted retreats. Then, beside them, [is] a hall, larger than need be for the purposes of a bath, but necessary for the reception of richer persons. Next, [large] locker rooms to undress in . . . with a very high and brilliantly lighted hall between them, in which are three swimming pools of cold water. On leaving this hall, you come to another [and] next to it [is] a very bright hall nicely fitted up for massage. . . . Near this is another hall, the most beautiful in the world, in which one can stand or sit [or stroll about] with comfort.

Lucian. *The Bath*. In *Roman Civilization: Selected Readings*. Volume 2, *The Empire*, edited by Naphtali Lewis and Meyer Reinhold. New York: Columbia University Press, 1990, pp. 140–141.

The Baths of Caracalla measured 1,107 by 1,104 feet. It could accommodate three thousand people and contained hot and cold pools, saunas, swimming pools, exercise areas, handball courts, reading rooms, snack bars, and shops. Paintings, statues, and mosaics adorned it.

form for new Christian churches (including Saint Peter's Basilica in Rome). At the same time, older basilicas were converted into churches. After the western Empire ceased to exist, Christianity survived, along with its many churches in the basilica form. Today, a majority of Christians are unaware that when they enter a cathedral they are in effect stepping through a doorway into the past. Indeed, this is only one of several ways that the monumental art of ancient Rome still exerts influence over the hearts and minds of millions of people.

Aqueducts, Water Systems, and Bridges

A mphitheaters, circuses, bathhouses, basilicas, and other huge buildings were without doubt among the Romans' most notable architectural achievements. Yet they were not the only giant structures that Rome produced. Aqueducts, water distribution systems, and bridges also exemplified the distinctive Roman art of building on a vast scale in order to meet practical needs. Although Rome's water systems, including aqueducts, were enormous constructions, they were located mostly underground and so were not readily visible. Partly for that reason they did not make it onto the many ancient lists of the so-called wonders of the world. But the famous first-century-A.D. Roman scholar Pliny the Elder had no doubts on that score, declaring:

> If we ponder the abundant water supply in public buildings, baths, open channels, private houses, gardens, and country estates; if we consider the distances traveled by [the] water [carried by the aqueducts], the building of the arches, the tunneling through mountains, and the construction of level routes across valleys, we can only conclude that this is a supreme wonder of the world.[26]

The Demand for Fresh Water

Before the Romans began building immensely complex water systems, they exploited the same simple water sources that all human societies had before them. These included streams, rivers, wells, and cisterns. The latter are artificial reservoirs for collecting and storing rainwater, which the Romans most often placed on rooftops. As the populations of Rome and other cities in the Empire grew increasingly large in the mid-to-late Republic, however, the demand for fresh water increased. It became necessary to bring extra supplies of water into the cities. So the Romans started building aqueducts, channels that carry water from one place to another. They also began installing elaborate systems to clean and distribute the water once it had reached the cities.

The Cisternone, built by Septimius Severus, is below the Castelli Romani in Rome. It is just one of many such cisterns that the Romans built to help ensure Rome's water supply.

Earlier peoples, including the Babylonians and Greeks, had built aqueducts. But as was often the case, though they were not very original, the Romans were determined, ingenious, daring, and extremely hardworking. In time, their water systems far surpassed any that had come before. Pliny's contemporary, Sextus Julius Frontinus, water commissioner for Rome in the late first century A.D., bragged, "With such an array of indispensable structures carrying so many waters, compare, if you will, the idle [Egyptian] Pyramids or the useless, though famous, works of the Greeks!"[27]

Frontinus's boast was well founded. Between 312 B.C. and A.D. 226, the Romans constructed eleven aqueducts to bring life-giving water into the capital city alone. (The Empire as a whole had more than six hundred of these structures.) Those eleven aqueducts covered a distance of more than 260 miles (418km), of which only about 29 miles (47km) carried the water above the ground, via tall rows of stone arches, an architectural form known as an arcade, or viaduct. (Basically bridges that supported the water channels, the arcades are today often confused with the aqueducts themselves.)

Building an Aqueduct

The first step in creating an aqueduct was to lay out a route running from the chosen water source (such as a lake, river, or mountain stream) to the target city. That path was often purposely indirect, with several twists and turns. The reason was that in order to make the water move through the channel, or *specus* (SPECK-us), the builders needed to take advantage of the natural effects of gravity. To that end, they slanted the channel very slightly—just enough to cause the water to flow downward from its source. The degree of incline varied from place to place, but averaged about 2 to 3 feet per mile (38cm to 57cm per km). To maintain the channel's gradual descent, it was necessary to overcome obstacles and changes in the terrain along the route. So an aqueduct frequently zigzagged across the countryside instead of following a straight line.

Once the surveyors had inspected the land, taken measurements, determined the proper route, and laid down wooden

The Roman aqueduct at Point du Gard, France, spans the Gardon River. The Romans built more than six hundred aqueducts throughout their empire.

stakes to mark that route, gangs of workers moved in. Their initial task was to clear away rocks, trees, and other obstructions. Next they dug trenches and tunnels to hold the *specus* and erected the arcades that would carry it across low-lying areas. These laborers were mainly free men who lived in the towns along the route, although the most arduous and dangerous jobs, like tunneling through hills, were likely given to slaves. (It was not cost-effective to have slaves do all the work. The expense of feeding, housing, and guarding them was practically the same as paying local workers, who were also more reliable and productive than slaves.)

FINDING THE PUREST WATERS

In ancient times, chemical treatment and other water purification methods did not yet exist. So when constructing aqueducts, the Romans tried to select the purest water sources possible. In his famous book, the noted first-century Roman architect Vitruvius told about the methods his countrymen employed to test the purity of such sources.

The discovery and testing of springs is to be pursued in the following manner. [If] they are strong, of clear complexion [appearance], free from distortion and inflamed eyes, the water will pass. If a fresh spring be dug, and the water, being sprinkled over a vessel of . . . good bronze, leave no trace [of residue], the water is very good. Or if water is boiled in a copper vessel and is allowed to stand and then poured off, it will also pass the test, if no sand or mud is found in the bottom. . . . [Also] if vegetables being put in the vessel with water and boiled are soon [i.e., rapidly] cooked, they will show that the water is good and wholesome.

Vitruvius. *On Architecture*. Vol. 2. Translated by Frank Granger. Cambridge, MA: Harvard University Press, 2002, pp. 177–179.

Where the ground was soft, the workers used shovels to dig the trenches. Then stonemasons cut stone slabs, which the workers used to construct a rectangular conduit, similar to a sewer tunnel, in the trenches. (Sometimes cement was used instead of or in addition to stone.) The average conduit was about 3 or 4 feet (1m) wide and almost twice that high. The tops of the conduits "were of three main types," scholars L.A. Hamey and J.A. Hamey explain, "flat slabs, twin slabs leaning against each other to form a pointed arch, and half-round arches."[28] When the route passed over rocky areas, where possible the workers employed picks, hammers, and chisels to carve the channel out of the naturally existing stone.

In those places where the *specus* emerged from the ground and laid atop an arcade, the stone arches were erected in the same way they were in other Roman buildings. The builders first made sure the foundation was level. Then they raised piers composed of stacks of stones and joined them with graceful arches. Sometimes only a few arches were required. But in some cases the arcades were very long and visually impressive, as in the case of the Aqua Claudia, erected in A.D. 38 and today the best preserved of Rome's eleven aqueducts. The section that carried the channel to the city walls had more than one thousand arches.

The System's Front End

When an aqueduct was completed, it consisted essentially of a miles-long watercourse with back and front ends. The back end was where the channel began in a lake, river, or other water source located somewhere in the countryside. The front end of the aqueduct was the complex system of pipes, holding tanks, fountains, and other facilities that distributed the water to the city's residents.

That system's daily output, that is, the number of gallons it supplied, varied from city to city. The general consensus of modern scholars for the total output of Rome's eleven aqueducts is about 250 million gallons (946 million L) a day. In the third century A.D., the city had approximately 1 million inhabitants, so the water system supplied each of them with about 250 gallons (946L) of water per day. Compare that amount with the roughly 125 gallons (469L) per person per day supplied by the average modern American city.

The front end of each of Rome's eleven aqueducts had a distribution building. It was situated on the highest point in the area so that the water would flow downward from it into the town. When the water from the *specus* entered the distribution building, it went directly into a large holding tank. There sediments and other impurities were removed by metal screens perforated by numerous small holes, and also by allowing the water to sit long enough for most impurities to settle to the bottom of the tank. (Workers emptied and cleaned the tanks on a regular basis.)

After cleaning, the water entered pipes made of materials ranging from wood and baked clay (ceramics) to bronze, lead, leather, and even concrete. Metal pipes, especially lead ones, were preferred because they were strong and reliable. However, they were also more expensive than other types, and fashioning them required specially trained artisans. Typically such an artisan heated a piece of lead until it was soft, rolled it into thin sheets, wrapped each sheet around a circular wooden dowel, sealed the seams with liquid lead, and allowed the lead to harden. To join two lengths of pipe, the artisan wrapped a metal collar around the junction and closed its seams with hot lead.

Contrary to some modern claims, the Romans were not unaware that lead pipes and containers can be hazardous to human health. Vitruvius was only one ancient writer who called attention to this problem. Water "seems to be made injurious by lead,"

A Roman water distribution system. Water comes out of the conduit in the ground into a pool that has channels cut into it and pipes placed to distribute water to various parts of the city.

he said, "therefore it seems that water should not be brought in lead pipes if we desire to have it [be] wholesome."[29] However, such warnings were not the main reason that the Romans eventually replaced many lead water pipes with ceramic ones. The changeover was more the result of the rising cost of lead. Vitruvius himself pointed out the cost-saving benefits, saying, "If we wish to employ a less expensive method, we must [use] earthenware pipes."[30]

Whatever the pipes were made of, they spread outward from the distribution building to various parts of the city. As a rule, they were buried roughly 2 feet (0.6m) beneath the pavement. Most of the water they carried ended up in public fountains, which in Rome were spaced an average of 260 feet (79m) apart. These were intended as aesthetic (artistic) creations and as places for citizens to draw their daily water supplies, which they scooped up in buckets.

The technology for allowing people to have running water in their homes did exist. Indeed, some of the shops and apartments on the ground floors of multistoried residential buildings in Rome did have running water, which flowed from bronze faucets not much different than those in modern kitchens and bathrooms. Most average Romans dwelled in the upper stories of such structures, however. Unfortunately for them, the pressure in the water systems of that age was not high enough to carry the water to the upper floors.

Fraud in the System

A further obstacle kept most Romans, including many who lived in one-story dwellings, from availing themselves of running water from the system. Namely, there were laws against running pipes from the aqueducts directly to private homes without special permission. "No one shall draw water from the public supply without a license," Frontinus reported. "Whoever wishes to draw water for private use must seek for a grant and bring to the [water] commissioner a writing [official permit] from the emperor."[31] Not surprisingly, society's wealthy and well-connected took advantage of their high positions to

One of the major reasons that so much is known about the ancient Roman aqueducts is that in A.D. 97 the emperor Nerva appointed a new imperial water commissioner. The man he chose was Sextus Julius Frontinus (circa 30–104), an honest, hardworking public official who was also a competent and prolific writer. Frontinus later described what he had learned about Rome's water system in a book titled The Aqueducts of Rome. The work is loaded with information that tells modern historians how the aqueducts, including their complex front ends, were constructed, how they were maintained, and even the daily output of each of Rome's life-giving water channels. In the introduction to the book, Frontinus makes clear the kind of detail he plans to present, saying:

I will first set down the names of the waters which enter the City of Rome. Then I will tell by whom, under what consuls, and in what year after the founding of the city each one was brought in; then at what point and at what milestone each water was taken, how far each is carried in a subterranean channel, how far on substructures, [and] how far on arches. Then I will give the elevation of each [and] how many public reservoirs there are, and from these how much [water] is delivered to public works, how much to ornamental fountains [and so forth].

Sextus Julius Frontinus. *The Aqueducts of Rome*. In *The Stratagems and the Aqueducts of Rome*, translated by C.E. Bennett. Cambridge, MA: Harvard University Press, 1993, pp. 331, 333, 335.

Frontius wrote The Aqueducts of Rome to describe how the aqueducts were built, maintained, and carried the city's daily intake of water.

obtain water licenses. Besides the emperors themselves, therefore, senators, members of noble families, owners of large businesses, military leaders, and close friends or associates of these privileged few had their own private water lines and all the running water they wanted.

Despite the rules that tightly regulated private use of water from the aqueducts, some individuals illegally ran pipes from various points in the water system to their homes. Sometimes they got away with it by bribing maintenance workers or officials of the water commission. The problem was pervasive enough to shock Frontinus when he inspected the system shortly after becoming water commissioner. He described this "fraud," as he called it, in his book about the aqueducts. "The cause of this," he said,

> is the dishonesty of the water-men [hired by former water commissioners], whom we have detected diverting water from the public conduits for private use. But a large number of landowners also, past whose fields the aqueducts run, tap the conduits. [We] have found irrigated fields, shops, garrets [houses of prostitution] and lastly [private] houses fitted up with fixtures through which a constant supply of flowing water might be assured.[32]

Like most Romans, Frontinus assumed that the aqueducts, along with Rome's other monumental architectural works, would endure virtually forever. When he passed away in A.D. 103, he could not foresee the Empire's collapse fewer than four centuries later. From that point on, with no more central government, including the water commission and its maintenance crews, the aqueducts fell increasingly into disrepair. A few underwent marginal repairs by Rome's medieval inhabitants. But this occurred in a haphazard, inadequate manner. So by about the year 1000, all eleven water channels had become inoperative. As their distant ancestors had before the rise of Roman engineering, people in the area resorted to drawing their water from the nearby Tiber River.

A Lasting Achievement

Another of Rome's great architectural forms, the stone bridge, both visually and structurally resembled the arcades that carried the aqueduct's water channels across valleys and plains. The main difference was that bridges carried people, animals, and wagons across rivers and other obstacles. Roman bridges were so well built and sturdy that some of them remain in use today and easily support the enormous weight of hundreds of cars, trucks, and other vehicles. Colin O'Connor, a leading authority on Roman bridges, calls them "one of the most successful, extensive, and lasting of all human, material achievements."[33]

Rome's earliest bridges were made of wood. One of the first and most famous, the Pons Sublicius, erected during the Monarchy, connected the Tiber's west bank with southwestern Rome. Many other timber bridges were built in the centuries

This model depicts Julius Caesar's engineering construction methods used to build the bridge over the Rhine River in 55 B.C.

The Roman bridge that spans the Tagus River in Spain is still in use today, a testament to Roman engineering.

that followed, some by and for the army, and others by local towns and individuals. A few were extremely impressive engineering feats.

Notable, for instance, was the one erected in 55 B.C. by the famous statesman and military general Julius Caesar. Spanning the Rhine River, on Germany's western border, it was intended to overawe the Germans by showing that the Romans could cross the river and attack them any time they wanted. The bridge was about 40 feet (12m) wide, 1,500 feet (458m) long, and took only ten days to complete.

Caesar chose to employ timber because he needed to create the bridge as fast as possible and with the materials that existed in the area. By his time, however, the Romans had been building stone bridges for more than two centuries. As was the case with all of Rome's monumental structures, the initial step in erecting a bridge was to provide a firm foundation for the piers. Sometimes the ground beneath the bridge was made of solid rock. If so, the piers would be well supported. But quite often the ground was soft, which was almost always the case when it was beneath a river. That called for fabricating a foundation from concrete. One fortunate boon was that Roman concrete hardened underwater, making it perfect for this kind of job. When the concrete foundation was hard enough, the workers installed the stone piers. If the bridge was on dry land, this was done in the usual way.

In contrast, if the bridge spanned a river, the workers had to remove the water first. This was accomplished using an apparatus called a coffer dam. In simple terms, it was a large wooden box having no top or bottom and sides that were watertight. Using a crane, workers lowered the box into the water, making sure that its top sections remained a few feet above the water's surface. Next, they removed the water from the box using buckets or a water screw (a corkscrew-like gadget that carried water upward when it was turned). When the ground inside the dam was dry, the workers began erecting the piers and arches. Eventually, these structural elements grew higher than the water level, at which point the dam was removed. The rest of the work was done on scaffolding attached to the exposed sections.

Finally, the builders laid down the roadway on top of the completed arches. If the single arcade was high enough in a given situation, the bridge was complete. If more height was required, a second or even a third arcade could be added to the first. The most famous Roman bridge, the magnificent Pont du Gard in southern France near Nimes, has such a three-tiered stack of arcades. With occasional minor repairs, it remained in use well into modern times.

As it turned out, the Pont du Gard and other large-scale Roman monuments served two purposes in their long history. The first was practical—to provide a place for chariot races or staging plays, or to carry water or to allow people to cross rivers. The second function served by Rome's monumental structures has been to stand, in silent majesty, as timeless memorials to their creators. Their mighty remains bear witness to that unique mixture of practicality, artistic sensibility, daring, and unflagging resolve possessed by Roman architects, engineers, and builders.

4

Roads, the "True Art of Rome"

Most modern experts agree with historian Edith Hamilton's famous assessment of ancient Rome's system of roads. She called it the "true art of Rome."[34] Both poetically and accurately, her words capture that singular sector of the Romans' spirit as a people that were driven to express their artistic inclinations on a grand scale.

Certainly the Roman road system, viewed in its entirety as a single piece of work, made all other architectural and artistic efforts in human history look puny in comparison. By A.D. 300 the Roman Empire possessed more than 300 partially or fully paved major highways that together stretched no less than 53,000 miles (85,295km). Moreover, thousands of smaller roads branched outward from these highways. Altogether, some scholars estimate, the Roman road system eventually extended over hundreds of thousands of miles. In the words of the noted twentieth-century historian Lionel Casson:

> The web of roads that Rome spun the length and breadth of the territory she administered was not only a magnificent achievement, but one of profound significance. It enabled her rulers to establish and maintain the most durable empire in European history; it set the

lines along which traders, priests, and soldiers would carry the seeds of change in Western civilization; it determined where many of the great urban centers of Europe were to be. Only a rich and powerful state whose authority stretched unchallenged far and wide could have . . . built so many thousands of miles of highway, maintained them more or less in good order, fitted them with the appropriate facilities, and given them the essential police protection.[35]

Compared with Earlier Road Builders

As was the case in most of their architectural and artistic work, the Romans did not invent large-scale road systems. The first to create such works were the Assyrians, a warlike Mesopotamian people who reached their height of power and prosperity in the late second and early first millennia B.C. The vast majority of Assyrian roads were made of dirt.

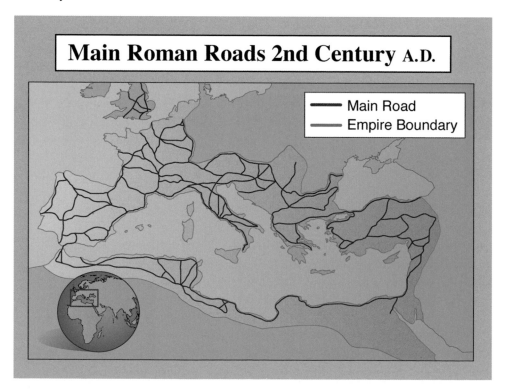

Main Roman Roads 2nd Century A.D.

— Main Road
— Empire Boundary

After the collapse of the Assyrian Empire in the late seventh century B.C., the Persian Empire arose in its place and eventually stretched from Afghanistan in the east to Anatolia (now Turkey) in the west. The Persians expanded and improved the Assyrian roads. Persian builders also created the so-called Royal Road, which achieved a length of roughly 1,600 miles (2,576km) as it connected the Persian capital of Susa to Sardis, a town in western Anatolia.

Farther west, in Italy during the Roman Monarchy, both the Greeks and Etruscans built some excellent roads using methods that Roman road builders would later copy. Those pre-Roman Italian roads were composed of dirt that had been well graded, packed down hard, and sometimes surfaced with gravel. They were also well maintained and drained of water after large rainstorms. The Romans built the same kind of high-quality dirt roads during the early years of the Republic.

The factor that separated Roman roads from those of the Greeks, Etruscans, and other ancient peoples was the addition of paving. Most often it consisted of small slabs of stone laid down atop carefully prepared roadbeds. Although paving stones had been used in Mesopotamia long before Roman times, they had covered only a few short stretches of road, each usually less than 1 mile (1.6km) long, mainly in the approaches to major temples. In comparison, the Romans applied stone paving to thousands of miles of roads.

Building a Road

The first major paved road the Romans built was the Via Appia, or Appian Way, named for its chief political sponsor, Appius Claudius. (*Via*, the Latin word most often used to describe large-scale Roman roads, meant a road wide enough for two vehicles—wagons or chariots—to pass each other.) Begun in 312 B.C. it eventually stretched from Rome to Brundisium (in southeastern Italy), a total of 370 miles (596km). The first-century-A.D. Roman poet Statius famously called it the Queen of Roads. Also, the sixth-century-A.D. Byzantine historian Procopius said of it, "The breadth of this road is such that

Building a Roman road. Surveyors mark out the route as workers build the road behind them.

two wagons going in opposite directions can pass one another, and it is one of the noteworthy sights of the world."[36]

The first step in building a major road such as the Via Appia was to lay out the proposed route, a job accomplished by surveyors. Once they had decided where the various straight stretches, twists, and turns would be, they marked the route with wooden stakes. The gangs of workers tasked with clearing the course of rocks, trees, and other impediments followed the lines of stakes.

Next a group of experienced workers began preparing the roadbed. As the aqueduct builders did, they dug trenches that would later be filled with various materials. The question of how deep to dig, or whether to dig at all, depended on the nature of the soil and terrain in a given area. If a section of road was slated to pass over a patch of ground that was rocky or otherwise very firm, no serious digging was required. The workers simply leveled the surface and set the paving stones right on the ground.

In contrast, sometimes the surveyors had no choice but to lay out a route that passed through soft and marshy or sandy regions. In such cases, Casson writes,

> the road gangs had to go to great lengths to prepare a proper bed. One way was to open a deep trench and simply toss in rock until so ponderous a load of stone had been laid down that a firm bed resulted. Where this would not work, they drove in wooden piers, brought in the carpenters to fashion a [horizontal] grillwork of wood [over the piers], and then laid a gravel road over the wood.[37]

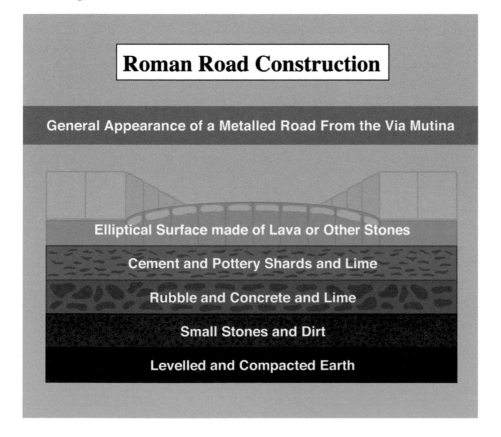

Roman Road Construction

General Appearance of a Metalled Road From the Via Mutina

Elliptical Surface made of Lava or Other Stones

Cement and Pottery Shards and Lime

Rubble and Concrete and Lime

Small Stones and Dirt

Levelled and Compacted Earth

Most stretches of road did not involve these two extremes of hard and soft, however. In the average situation, the workers dug a trench 2 to 5 feet (0.6m to 1.5m) deep, at which point they usually reached a layer where the ground was firm enough. Then they poured in a layer of fill composed of a mixture of clay and rounded fieldstones. Depending on the individual situation, that much might be enough. Or more layers—one or more of clay alone, one or more of rocks alone, and maybe another mixture of the two—might be needed.

Surfaces and Special Features

To this reinforced roadbed, the builders finally laid down the all-important road surface. In some roads, including selected stretches of major highways like the Via Appia, a layer of hard-packed gravel was deemed sufficient. The compacting was done by animals or groups of men dragging large stone rollers over the surface several times.

In the case of paved road stretches, the stones were cut into either rectangles, which abutted one another at right angles; or irregular polygons, which fit together like the pieces of a jigsaw puzzle. The lengthy paved sections of the Via Appia utilized the polygonal approach, and the builders fitted these stones together with amazing precision. After inspecting that renowned road more than six centuries after it was paved, an astonished Procopius said:

> After working these stones until they were smooth and flat, and cutting them to a polygonal shape, [the builders] fastened them together without putting concrete or anything else between them. And they were fastened together so securely and the joints were so firmly closed, that they give the appearance, when one looks at them, not of being fitted together, but of having *grown* together. And after the passage of so long a time, and after being traversed by many wagons and all kinds of animals every day [for centuries], they have neither separated at all at the joints, nor has any one of the stones been worn out or reduced in thickness,—

The chief figure behind Rome's first major and most famous road, the Via Appia, or Appian Way, was Appius Claudius (circa 340–273 B.C.). A noted Roman politician, he served as consul, or chief state administrator-general, twice (307 and 296 B.C.) and as dictator, or emergency leader, twice (292 and 285 B.C.). His road-related work occurred in 312 B.C. when he was serving as censor, a public official in charge of the census and of awarding contracts for public construction projects. Taking direct control of the Via Appia, named for him, Appius hired the engineers and foremen, who in turn organized the work gangs to get the project off the ground. Appius Claudius also gained fame for initiating Rome's first

aqueduct, also named for him—the Aqua Appia. The great first-century-B.C. Roman historian Livy wrote, "For later generations, the name of Appius was of happier memory because he built a road and brought a water supply into the city. He was solely responsible for these achievements because his colleagues had resigned office, [leaving him to continue] to hold the censorship alone."

Livy. *History of Rome from Its Foundation.* In *Livy: Rome and Italy,* translated by Betty Radice. New York: Penguin, 1982, pp. 257–258.

The Via Appia outside Rome. Appius Claudius built the Appian Way starting in 312 B.C. The road is still in use today.

nay, they have not even lost any of their polish. Such, then, is the Appian Way![38]

Whatever method the builders chose to surface their roads, all the major ones had a number of special features. One of the more important was cambering, in which the middle of the road was slightly higher than the sides. As one expert explains, this was done

> so that rainwater would quickly drain away from the surface. A gentle slope on either side of the road then led the water to a ditch, usually two or three meters (7–10 feet) away, over ground which had been cleared of vegetation. [Without cambering] both surface and foundations [of a road] will be broken up if water is allowed to stand on the road and then to sink through into the soil below.[39]

The larger Roman highways, particularly their portions near cities, also featured artificial ruts carved into their surfaces. Their purpose was to guide the wheels of carts and chariots and thereby ensure they would not skid in rainy weather, when the roads were slippery. Another special feature consisted of high, flat-topped stones placed at intervals along the roadside. These allowed mounted travelers who had climbed off their horses to mount them again with greater ease. (Stirrups, which aid a person climbing onto a horse, had not yet been invented.) Finally, the builders installed milestones (*miliaria*), one for each Roman mile (measuring 4,995 feet, or 1,523 meters, compared to 5,280 feet, or 1,610 meters, in a modern mile). These signposts told travelers the distances between towns along the road.

Couriers of the Government Post

Horse-mounting aids and milestones were among numerous amenities that were added to Rome's more traveled roads over

the course of several centuries. Others include inns, stables, blacksmith shops, places to eat, market stands, small chapels, and more. Such services had the effect of making travel on the roads both more convenient and more appealing. This naturally increased the number of travelers and in turn led to the growth of new villages and towns along these routes. A leading expert on Roman roads, Raymond Chevallier, writes:

> A road attracts people for a variety of reasons—sightseeing, excitement, news and novelty, useful ideas and information, fashions and slogans, [and] the variety of

A Roman relief of a mail carrier from Maria Saal, Austria. The Roman emperor Augustus organized a regular courier and mail service throughout the Empire.

goods on offer. The fact that people could satisfy each other's needs and move easily around was the key to the many-sided development of town life. The initial grouping of population centered on the road was followed by a second phase in which there grew up a system of scattered settlements linked by short antennae [minor roads] to the main road.[40]

One way that the Roman roads caused scattered towns and other settlements to work together in an ordered system benefiting all citizens of the Empire was through the government

HOW SOLDIERS USED THE ROADS

The better-built and longer Roman roads were at first built in large part to allow Roman soldiers to move through the countryside with as much speed and efficiency as possible. In his lengthy history of Rome, the first-century-B.C. Roman historian Livy tells how, during a countrywide emergency in the late third century B.C., the Roman dictator Fabius and his leading officers used the Via Flaminia, a well-built road running northward from Rome, to join forces with one of the consuls and his soldiers. The worried Fabius was relieved when he saw "the consul riding towards him with his cavalry"[1] along the road. In another passage, Livy describes the situation that existed after a bloody battle had raged on Roman soil. Officials in the capital sent "wagons and pack-animals" along the larger roads "to aid in the transport of men, exhausted as they were by fighting and by marching all night." Then a Roman general ordered messengers "to the towns along the Appian Way," telling them "to have supplies ready within their own walls, and also to bring them down to the [main] road from the outlying farms [along the smaller roads]."[2]

1. Livy. *History of Rome from Its Foundation*. In Livy: *The Early History of Rome*, translated by Aubrey de Sélincourt. New York: Penguin, 2002, p. 314.
2. Livy, *History*. In *Livy: The War with Hannibal*, translated by Aubrey de Sélincourt. New York: Penguin, 1987, pp. 106, 365.

post (*cursus publicus*). During the centuries of the Republic, both military generals and government officials had sent out riders carrying messages, news, and other vital information. This was done in an irregular, piecemeal fashion, however. It was not until the first Roman emperor, Augustus, took charge of the realm in the late first century B.C. that a more organized and regular courier service—the post—was established.

Some of the messengers traveled in horse-drawn carriages. This is known because archaeologists found a carved scene on a gravestone that shows an official courier sitting in a carriage drawn by three horses. He wears a hooded cloak and holds a riding crop. Beside him sits his servant, who is apparently helping to guard the bags containing the letters and other materials they are transporting. Such a carriage could cover about 30 to 45 miles (48km to 72km) a day, depending on the lay of the land, the quality of the road, and the weather. Messages that needed to get to their destinations as fast as possible were almost certainly carried by single mounted riders. The best of them could cover 130 miles (209km) or more in a day.

Posting Stations and Inns

Aiding the couriers, as well as merchants, tourists, religious pilgrims, and other travelers, were a variety of facilities that dotted the main roads. One consisted of small posting stations, places where someone could get a fresh horse or have his carriage repaired if needed. Travelers could also obtain food for themselves and their animals. These stations were located about 7 to 12 miles (11km to 19km) apart.

Inns also grew up along the larger roads, on average one every 20 to 30 miles (32km to 48km). Ordinary travelers, as well as couriers, availed themselves of these facilities, which featured both food and beds for the night. Such inns were owned and run by private businessmen rather than the government. The most common arrangement was for the innkeeper to allow the official couriers to stay for free in exchange for the right to build and operate near a major road and take advantage of its heavy traffic to find customers.

A number of ancient literary sources mention or describe these lodging houses that dotted the Roman roads. Also archaeologists have found and studied the remains of several—in Rome, Pompeii, and towns in France, Germany, and other parts of Europe. So historians know a fair amount about them and their varied amenities and services. The names of the inns, for example, were frequently quite quaint or charming. Some utilized gods' names, like "The Mercury and Apollo," or "The Diana," while others leaned toward animals—"The Little Eagle," "The Elephant," "The Serpent"—or everyday objects—"The Sword," "The Wheel."

Having a colorful name was not the only way to attract customers, however. Innkeepers often placed signs or plaques outside their establishments in hopes of drawing in travelers. The plaque that stood outside the Mercury and Apollo, in what is now Lyons, France, reads, "Here, Mercury [patron deity of travelers] promises you wealth, Apollo [god of healing] health, and Septumanus [the innkeeper] room and board. Whoever comes [inside] will be the better for it afterwards. Traveler, keep an eye on where you will [stay]!"[41]

The layout of most Roman roadside inns appears to have been fairly standard, although there were considerable differences in size. Most of those in Pompeii had fewer than a dozen rooms for rent, whereas one found in Rome had more than thirty. An inn unearthed by archaeologists in Austria was 70 feet (21m) long, 40 feet (12m) wide, and had two floors. On the ground floor was an open courtyard in which guests parked carriages and wagons, a stable to board travelers' horses, a blacksmith's forge, a large kitchen, and a dining room. The bed chambers for guests were on the second floor.

Another Roman inn was discovered in Neuss, Germany, in 2004. Based on the evidence she has gathered to date, the director of excavations, Sabine Sauer, describes some of the services the place offered. "Upon arrival," she says,

> travelers would have entered a forecourt, where mechanics stood by at a chariot service station. Hay and water troughs would have given the horses a nibble and

a drink while their owners dined on a variety of foods, including ethnic cuisine. . . . We know from the bones [we found in the inn's rubbish heap] that they ate a lot of meat—chicken and pork—as well as bread, rice, lentils and fruit. There were desserts of sweet cakes, cooked with sesame seeds and almonds. There must have been a flourishing trade; there were many fragments of wine amphora [storage jars] and broken plates.[42]

The combination of extensive services along the roads, the skills and dogged determination of the builders, and the sheer numbers and lengths of the Roman roads made them still another unsung wonder of the ancient world. Moreover, their

ROMAN ROAD GUIDES

The Romans had road guides similar in many ways to modern ones. These pamphlet-like books, called *itineraria*, cited the distances from city to city and the locations of inns, posting stations, stables, guest-houses, and other facilities along the roads. A handful of these guides have survived. One dating to the early fourth century A.D., when Christianity was steadily gaining standing and popularity in the Empire, was written for religious pilgrims. It indicates the best roads to take from towns in Gaul (now France) across southern Europe to Jerusalem, in Palestine, which the Christians already considered a sacred city. The section of the guide that shows Gaul contains almost 400 miles (644km) of roads and singles out eleven inns and thirty posting stations. Similar guides existed for non-Christian Romans. There were also maps one could buy that not only showed the inns and other stopping places, but also rated them for quality, just as many modern guidebooks do.

An excavated Roman inn shows the *thermopilium*, or "fast food" area so common to Roman inns.

importance lived on long after the demise of the Roman realm itself. Medieval and early modern Europeans continued to tread those highways, and several remain in use today. The late historian of Roman culture F.R. Cowell concisely summed up the crucial legacy of the Roman roads when he said, "Of all Rome's material achievements, none did so much to aid the spread of civilization and culture, or the Romanization of the West than these roads."[43]

Painting, Mosaics, and Sculpture

By the mid-second century A.D., towns across the Mediterranean-European world ruled by Rome were filled with beautiful paintings, sculptures, and mosaics. Some were old, having been produced during Rome's republican era. But a great many had been made during the early years of the Empire, as Roman cities, public buildings, and even some houses tried to acquire a look of imperial splendor.

It is important to stress that a large portion of these artworks commissioned and exhibited by Romans were actually created by Greeks. Although long since conquered by Rome, the Greek lands had largely retained their native cultures and artistic traditions. Because the Romans grudgingly admired Greek culture and art, they frequently either hired Greek artists or utilized the services of Greeks who lived among them. (Some of the slaves and former slaves who worked for Roman homeowners or the Roman government were talented artists.)

Thus, only some, perhaps even a minority, of Roman paintings, mosaics, and sculptures produced during the Empire were created by Romans. Moreover, in those days almost no effort was made to differentiate among the artists' nationalities. That has made it difficult for modern scholars to tell exactly who created

what. This problem is further complicated by what was then a common custom among artists: not signing their works. As German scholar Ludwig Friedlander tells it: "A comparatively small number of the many thousands of artists who exercised their craft

This Roman fresco from Pompeii depicts a garden and birds. The Romans loved to fill the walls of their homes with scenes from the countryside.

during the early centuries of the Empire are known to us by name. . . . This is partly to be explained by the subordinate position held by artists in society. [They] were held, as individuals, in little regard."[44]

Painting Techniques and Pigments

Whatever the exact nationalities and names of Rome's artists, they produced an enormous number of works, many of which were of high quality. This can be seen in the enduring medium of painting. Almost all of the surviving Roman paintings are wall murals done in the fresco style, in which the paint is applied to a coating of wet plaster. In the first of the standard steps in ancient fresco painting, the artist applied two, three, or more thin layers of limestone plaster to the wall. Then he painted the background of the scene he intended to create. Such backgrounds often included large architectural forms—such as temples, arcades, and/or ornate Corinthian columns—dotting pleasant rural landscapes. (The Romans, who started out as rural agriculturalists, had a special fondness for idyllic images of the countryside.) In the next step, the painter added human and/or animal figures and other foreground details. When the mural was completely dry, he applied a layer of transparent glue or wax to create a bright, glossy, fairly resilient surface.

The pigments of the paints such artists used were made from various natural materials, especially minerals and animal and vegetable dyes. Red, for example, came from the mineral cinnabar (mercury sulfide), which people first heated and then dried and ground into a powder. Red ocher, made from iron oxides, was also used for red pigments. White came from chalk, marble dust, or oyster shells, and blue was made by combining copper filings with ground sand and baking the mixture. To create the paint itself, these and similar powdered pigments were mixed with appropriate amounts of liquids such as water, egg, or honey, along with animal glues or other sticky agents to help the paint bond well to the plaster surface.

Although wall murals were by far the most common type of Roman paintings, modern experts believe that other kinds utilized similar pigments, styles, and subjects. These included portable paintings, that is, those done on wood, canvas, and other materials that could be moved from place to place. The versions

A panel from a bedroom in Pompeii depicts a city scene. The Romans painted on wood, canvas, plaster, and other materials.

done on pieces of wood are known as panel paintings. A scholar at the New York Metropolitan Museum of Art explains:

> The history of Roman painting is essentially a history of wall paintings on plaster. Although ancient literary references inform us of Roman paintings on wood, ivory, and other materials, works that have survived are in the durable medium of fresco that was used to adorn the interiors of private homes in Roman cities and in the countryside. . . . Despite the lack of physical evidence, we can assume that many portable paintings depicted subjects similar to those found on the painted walls in Roman villas. It is also reasonable to suppose that Roman panel paintings, which included both original creations and adaptations of renowned [earlier Greek] works, were the prototypes for the myths depicted in [later Roman wall] frescoes. Roman artists specializing in fresco most likely traveled with copybooks that reproduced popular [Greek and other] paintings, as well as decorative patterns [so they could copy them when creating murals for new customers].[45]

The Buried Murals

The most numerous and complete surviving examples of Roman paintings are the wall murals found in the ruins of Pompeii and Herculaneum, which were buried by Mount Vesuvius's A.D. 79 eruption. The fact that so many finely fashioned paintings existed in these small cities suggests that such artworks were very common throughout the Empire. The murals also show that large numbers of Roman paintings were not isolated decorative pieces, as most modern framed paintings are. Instead, they frequently covered entire walls and showed life-size depictions of doors, windows, furniture, pillars, and so forth. In rooms having little furniture, these images were essential elements of the house's interior decor.

Also widespread were painted images of scenes from everyday life, landscapes, and mythical characters. Of the mythological scenes, one of the most striking was found in the

House of the Vettii (near the city's northern defensive wall and the gate named after Mount Vesuvius). The painting portrays the baby Hercules (the Roman version of the Greek Heracles, a famous legendary hero) fighting with serpents that an angry goddess had sent to kill him.

A particularly revealing landscape from Pompeii comes from the House of the Centenary (a few blocks southeast of

The Bacchus and Mount Vesuvius fresco painting was found during the excavation of the House of the Centenary in Pompeii.

the House of the Vettii). It depicts Mount Vesuvius with its preeruption cone still intact and covered with trees and lush vineyards. Bacchus, god of wine and fertility, stands nearby, covered in grapes, apparently content with the peaceful pastoral scene. It is clear from these images that the residents of Pompeii, and probably all Romans, were unaware that the seemingly serene mountain in their midst was actually a dangerous volcano about to blow its top.

One of the most significant and beautiful wall paintings unearthed at Pompeii was dubbed the "Lost Ram" by modern

HIGH-PLACED ART LOVERS

One reason that many well-to-do Romans commissioned artists to do paintings was that a number of noted politicians, generals, and other high-placed individuals promoted the arts. In this passage from his encyclopedic book, Natural History, the famous Roman scholar Pliny the Elder explains that the successful general Julius Caesar and his adopted son Octavian (later Augustus) were big painting enthusiasts.

It was the dictator Caesar who ensured outstanding official importance for [painted] pictures when he dedicated paintings of [the mythical characters] Ajax and Medea in front of the Temple of Venus. . . . [But] the late emperor Augustus surpassed all others when he put two pictures in the busiest part of the [main] Forum, one representing War and Triumph, the other Castor and Pollux together with Victory. Similarly, in a wall of the Senate House, which he was dedicating . . . he set a picture of [the minor goddess] Nemea seated on a lion, holding a palm-branch in her hand. Next to her stood an old man leaning on a stick. And above his head was a two-horse chariot.

Pliny the Elder. *Natural History*. In *Pliny the Elder: Natural History: A Selection*, translated by John H. Healy. New York: Penguin, 1991, p. 327.

scholars. (It is unknown which house it originally came from.) Unlike most other Roman murals, which are realistic in style, it has the sketchy, inexplicit look of modern impressionistic paintings and seems to foreshadow that style by many centuries. According to Michael Grant:

> The painting displays a landscape [in which] we see an idealized rustic shrine, located in rocky scenery containing trees. . . . In the foreground a man is guiding or pushing a ram or goat, covered with long hair, towards the shrine, as if for sacrifice. That is to say, despite the general tranquility of the scene . . . there is evidence of tension. . . . The painting is clever, clearly the work of a master of impressionism. The goat and herdsman are represented by a few well-chosen brush-strokes. [The figures] are projected like shadows upon the walls of the shrine, which are light-colored . . . [while] the rocks in the background seem to start dark gray, turn to purple-white, and finally gleam in purple-pink, as if the last rays of the sun were striking the mountainside. Subtle variations of mood and accent were attained.[46]

Other Popular Subjects

Although mythology and nature were frequent general themes in Roman painting, also popular were some forms and subjects that were very specific to Roman culture. One was known as the "triumphal painting." After gaining victory in a battle or war, a Roman general was accorded a special parade called a triumph, in which he and his soldiers, carrying the spoils they had captured, marched through the capital. It became customary to commission large paintings showing scenes from these conflicts. A vivid description of a series of such paintings was recorded by the first-century-A.D. Jewish historian Josephus. These "showed the successive stages of the war," he wrote.

> Here was to be seen a smiling countryside laid waste, there whole formations of the enemy put to the sword;

men in flight and men led off to captivity; walls of enormous size thrown down by [siege] engines; great strongholds stormed; cities whose battlements were lined with defenders overwhelmed; an army streaming inside a city], the whole place wreaking of slaughter. . . . The art and marvelous craftsmanship of these [paintings] revealed the incidents to those who had not seen them happen as clearly as if they had been there.[47]

Another typically Roman theme frequently depicted in paintings was gladiatorial combat. A number of examples of such artworks were found at Pompeii, as well as in several other excavations of Roman towns across Italy and the rest of Europe. In Pliny the Elder's words: "When a freedman [freed slave] of Nero was putting on a gladiatorial show at Antium, paintings containing life-like portraits of all the gladiators and their assistants decorated the public [squares]. Portraits of gladiators have commanded the greatest interest in art for many generations."[48]

Mosaics

The subjects and images of many popular Roman paintings were subsequently used as models for mosaics, which began to appear with some frequency in Italy in the second century B.C. In the centuries that followed, mosaics became standard decorations for floors, walls, and occasionally ceilings of both public and private buildings. These often stunning artworks were created by placing small stone, glass, or pottery cubes (*tesserae*) into wet cement and allowing it to dry.

For themes, some mosaics employed purely decorative abstract forms, such as repeated swirls, squares, triangles, and other geometric shapes and patterns. Other mosaics depicted realistic subjects, including landscapes, buildings, people, animals, and both mythical and historical events. One famous historical event captured in a large mosaic, measuring 19 by 10 feet (6 by 3m), was found in the House of the Faun in Pompeii. It shows the Macedonian Greek conqueror Alexander III (later called "the

Great") bearing down on the Persian king Darius III in the midst of the battle of Issus in 333 B.C. Modern experts estimate that some 1.5 million tiny pieces of colored stone and glass went into the original work, about two-thirds of which survives intact. They also believe that the mosaic was based directly on an earlier painting, now lost, by one of two Greek masters, Apelles or Philoxenos of Eretria.

A very fine example of a Roman floor mosaic depicting animals was discovered in 1996 in Lod, Israel. A spokesperson for the Metropolitan Museum of Art, where the mosaic was displayed in late 2010 and early 2011, says of it:

> Believed to belong to a large house owned by a wealthy Roman in about A.D. 300, the mosaic comprises a large square panel with a central medallion depicting various exotic animals and two rectangular end panels, one of which represents a marine scene of fish and ships. The floor, which adorned a richly appointed audience room, is extremely well preserved and highly colorful.[49]

This 19-by-10-foot mosaic was found in Pompeii and depicts the battle of Issus in 333 B.C. It has an estimated 1.5 million pieces of colored stone and glass.

This excellent example of Roman mosaic floors was unearthed in Israel in 1996.

Interestingly, some Roman mosaics served as maps as well as decorations. An example from what is now Jordan, in Palestine, dates from the mid-500s A.D., when, despite the recent fall of the western portion of the Empire, Roman lands in the East were still thriving. It is a huge work, measuring 79 by 20 feet (24m by 6m). "Its purpose," Lesley Adkins explains, "was to portray the Bible lands, and place names [in the mosaic] are in Greek. Jerusalem is shown in a larger scale than the surrounding area."[50]

Sculpture

Just as the styles and themes of many Roman paintings and mosaics were based on or influenced by Greek versions, much Roman sculpture borrowed heavily from Greek models. Nevertheless, the Romans did more than simply copy Greek figurines and statues. An area of sculpture in which they excelled and developed their own artistic voice was portraiture. Some of these portraits were free-standing statues and some were carved in relief, that is, projecting partially from a flat stone surface. However, the majority took the form of busts.

Roman portraits, including busts, initially emerged as a true art form in the third century B.C. and became most numerous and highly developed in the early Empire. The sculptors were extremely adept at expressing the personal characters of their subjects, often with unflattering accuracy. This individualistic approach contrasted sharply with that of the Greeks, whose sculptures more often depicted more generalized and frequently ideal forms and features.

Roman portraiture did not appear in a vacuum. Rather, it was in large degree based on a custom quite common during the Republic—fashioning highly realistic death masks (*imagines*) of deceased relatives. "Wax masks of members of their family," Pliny said of his ancestors, "were displayed on individual urns so that their likenesses might be carried in procession at family funerals. For, invariably, when someone died, all the members of his family who had ever existed were present [in the form of the masks]."[51]

Portrait busts and statues continued to develop during the remainder of the Republic, creating what one expert calls "an astonishing gallery of revealing images of men and women of all degree, from emperor to tradesman."[52] Increasingly during these years, politicians and other prominent men used them to promote their public images in the same way their modern

RECYCLED PORTRAIT BUSTS

As explained here by scholar Rosemarie Trentinella, of the Metropolitan Museum of Art, the Romans sometimes recycled, or recarved, portrait busts of public officials, including emperors, who had developed seedy or disreputable reputations.

I n the instance of the "bad" emperors such as Nero and Domitian, whose reigns were characterized by destructive behavior and who were posthumously condemned by the Senate, imperial portraits were sometimes recycled or even destroyed. Typical effects of . . . the most severe denunciation included the erasure of an individual's name from public inscriptions, and even assault on their portraits as if brought against the subject himself. Imperial portraits of "bad" emperors were also re-

moved from public view and warehoused, often later recycled into portraits of private individuals or emperors of the following decades. A recarved portrait is relatively easy to recognize. Certain features such as a disproportionate [badly proportioned] hairline or unusually flattened ears are typical signs that a bust had been altered from an earlier likeness.

Rosemarie Trentinella. *Roman Portrait Sculpture: Republican Through Constantinian.* Metropolitan Museum of Art. www.metmuseum.org/toah/hd/ropo/hd_ropo.htm.

This marble bust of the emperor Nerva was reworked from a bust of defamed emperor Domitian in the first century A.D.

counterparts do with appearances on TV, in magazines, and on the Internet. This practice reached its peak among the emperors, as explained by art historian Rosemarie Trentinella. After Augustus established the Empire, she writes,

> the imperial family and its circle soon came to monopolize official public statuary. Official imperial portrait types were principally displayed in [temples] and were carefully designed to project specific ideas about the emperor, his family, and his authority. These sculptures were extremely useful as propaganda tools intended to support the legitimacy of the emperor's powers. [Among]

The emperor Augustus built the Ara Pacis (Altar of Peace) between 13 and 9 B.C. Figures are carved in extraordinary detail around the outside of the altar.

the most influential, and most widely disseminated, media for imperial portraits [was] sculpture, and official types [of sculpture] laden with propagandistic [messages] were dispersed throughout the Empire to announce and identify the imperial authority.[53]

One of the climaxes of Roman portrait sculpture is represented by the numerous relief sculptures carved into the walls

POOR PUBLIC TASTES IN ART?

Widely different standards of what constitutes good or proper art have existed in every society, ancient and modern. A case in point was the apparently stuffy first-century-B.C. Roman architect Vitruvius. In this brief tract from his noted book, he complains that the public has recently developed what he views as poor tastes in art (because they have come to like many impressionistic and fanciful images rather than traditional realistic ones, which he is used to).

[The great paintings of the past] are now disdained by the improper taste of the present. [Pictures show fantastic] monsters rather than definite representations taken from definite things [i.e., reality]. Instead of columns, there rise up stalks [and] candelabra uphold pictured shrines [with] clusters of thin stalks . . . with little figures [of people] seated upon them at random [or] the heads of men and animals attached to half the body. Such things neither are, nor can be, nor have been [real]. On these lines the new fashions compel bad judges to condemn good craftsmanship for dullness. . . . Yet when people view these falsehoods, they approve rather than condemn, failing to consider whether any of them can really occur or not, [for] pictures cannot be approved which do not resemble reality!

Vitruvius. *On Architecture.* Vol. 2. Translated by Frank Granger. Cambridge, MA: Harvard University Press, 2002, p. 105.

of the *Ara Pacis* (Altar of Peace). This superlative monument, installed in Rome by Augustus, began construction in 13 B.C. and was inaugurated four years later. Shaped like a box, with an external stairway leading to a door to the altar inside, it is stunning in its simplicity. What immediately catches the eye is a formal parade of human figures, one of the emperor himself, carved in extraordinary detail on the outside of the box's walls. As Mortimer Wheeler describes it, some of the figures are

> engaged in conversation, [while] a veiled lady in the background, identified tentatively as the sister of Augustus, places her finger to her lips in silent rebuke to a couple who are chattering in the foreground. . . . [One of children depicted] grabs the toga of the man next to him [as if asking] to be picked up. But instances such as these are all subordinated to the overall dignity of the scene, in which contemporary living people, of whom several [including Augustus] can still be identified, are caught in marble, just as they were at a given moment on July 4, 13 B.C.[54]

The late historian Donald Dudley called the moment in which the *Ara Pacis* was dedicated the "high noon,"[55] or pinnacle, of the Roman Empire. The high noon of Roman art was yet to come, for many amphitheaters, bathhouses, basilicas, and other enormous architectural works had yet to be erected. Yet in that glorious moment when Augustus stood before his subjects on the altar's steps in 9 B.C., the Romans could boast that at last they had produced works of sculpture that could stand with those of the Greeks.

6

Ceramics, Metalwork, and Other Crafts

As remains the case today, in ancient times certain products were manufactured by skilled craftspeople. Among the more numerous and important categories of craftwork in the ancient Roman world were ceramics (pottery), metalworking, coin making, and glassmaking. Like craftspeople throughout much of history, Roman artisans in these disciplines turned out objects used by most people on a daily basis. Partly for this reason, the quality of work varied widely.

Some Roman pottery, for instance, was coarse, plain, and marketed to members of the lower classes, who could not afford better. Yet at the same time, other Roman potters turned out finely made, visually beautiful wares that deserve to be classified as art. The same can be said of a small but significant portion of the output of all Roman crafts. The proof for this takes the form of plentiful examples on display in major museums in Europe, the Middle East, North Africa, and the United States.

Ceramic Methods

Whether their wares were crude and cheap or exquisite and expensive, potters in the Roman-ruled lands created a wide range of widely used objects. These included drinking cups, bowls, pitchers, and other tableware; vases; cooking pots; storage containers; oil lamps and candlesticks; urns for human remains; figurines and ornaments; toys; tourist souvenirs; and many more. The number of such wares created over the course of the Roman realm's existence is impossible to determine. But experts agree that it must be staggeringly high. Indeed, ceramic articles are the most common artifacts unearthed at all Greco-Roman archaeological digs.

This clay pitcher in the shape of a rooster is from Pompeii. Roman potters created a wide variety of pottery for everyday use.

The exact manner in which Roman pottery was produced is still a bit unclear, in part because no Roman potter's wheels have survived. Also, ancient writers rarely described the methods involved. The general consensus of modern scholars is that a potter first mixed his clay with water to the desired firmness and made sure it was free from sand and other particles. Then he made the bowl, pitcher, or other pot in one of three ways—hand shaping, placing the clay in wooden or stone molds, or throwing it on a potter's wheel. The latter was by far the most prevalent method, especially in the production of finer pottery.

After the potter had shaped the object and allowed it to dry, he put it in a kiln and baked it at a high temperature. The kilns varied significantly in size. Some were fairly small, with a capacity for only a few pots, while others held dozens or even hundreds of objects. In towns or regions in which large ceramics industries developed, as one expert points out, "some kilns were enormous, holding up to 40,000 vessels."[56] After baking, some of these vessels were left plain, but others were painted with various designs, human and animal figures and flowers being the most common themes.

Pottery Types

Several different types of Roman pottery developed, depending on the regions where they were made and the markets they were aimed at. Some fell into the general category of native wares. Many native wares followed established styles that had developed in non-Roman lands before Rome had conquered them. Some were cheaply made, plain, and unpainted, while others, especially in a number of Greek areas, were of higher quality and beautifully decorated.

Another general category of ceramics in the late Republic and on into the Empire is called trade wares because the objects were distributed to most or all parts of the realm. The leading kind of Roman trade ware, particularly among finer ceramic products, was called *terra sigillata*. People also called such pots Samian wares, red-gloss wares, or red-coated wares, and in North Africa, red-slipped wares. As the name indicates,

This red-coated Arretine ware was made by the Roman potter P. Cornelius. New firing methods in the mid-first century B.C. brought about the first red-coated ware.

POTTERY HELPS IN DATING SITES

*A*rchaeologists frequently use the Roman pottery known as *terra sigillata* to aid in dating the sites in which examples of it are found. The physical forms and decorative styles of such pots underwent small but regular changes over time. Also, the potters frequently signed their pots by stamping them with their names or other marks. Experts have determined which forms, styles, potters, and in some cases even individual workshops existed in each succeeding era. So if they find a specific kind of pot in a certain layer of a dig, they can date that layer with fair accuracy. Archaeologist Roy A. Adkins comments on the potters' stamps: "*Terra sigillata* is useful for dating because . . . most of the vessels bear potters' name stamps, [and] the mold maker's name was sometimes present, usually incised with a stylus [thin, pointed tool] as a signature in the mold, so that a mirror image appeared on the vessel. On decorated vessels, stamps advertising the workshop were often used."

Lesley Adkins and Roy A. Adkins. *Handbook to Life in Ancient Rome.* New York: Facts On File, 2004, p. 316.

A terra sigillata *bowl from the first century* A.D. Terra sigillata *is useful for dating pottery because most vessels have the potter's or mold maker's name incised on the piece.*

most red-coated wares possessed a reddish color, in part because they were made from red clays.

This popular type of Roman pottery originally developed from imitations of fine Greek ceramics. In the fourth century B.C., Roman potters started copying Greek vases, urns, and other pots that utilized reddish-hued clays. The most prevalent early Italian adaptation came to be called Campanian ware because so many of the artisans who made it worked in Campania, a region centered in west coastal Italy. This style underwent relatively minor changes for a long time. Eventually, however, in the mid-first century B.C. (during the civil wars that ended up destroying the Republic), new firing methods began to be used. This development brought about the introduction of the first red-coated ware, which was initially referred to as Arretine ware after the town in which it originated—Arretium (modern Arezzo), in central Italy. A fine surviving example is a high-handled water jug from the early first century A.D., now on display in London's prestigious British Museum. According to a museum scholar:

> The lower body of the jug is decorated with motifs in sharp relief. Contained within two horizontal bands of concentric circles is a zig-zag pattern of straight festoons [garlands] with rosettes [rose-like ornaments] at the angles. Above the festoons are ivy leaves and rosettes, while below are straight elongated leaves and tendrils. In the upper part of the decoration is a name stamp of P. Cornelius, one of the most famous "Arretine" potters of the period. The pottery jug's debt to [imitation of] metalwork can be seen in details of the form, such as the foot, the high, arching handle and in particular the way in which the handle is attached to the body.[57]

In the final decades of the first century B.C., Italian merchants spread Arretine ware across the Mediterranean lands into Palestine, Syria, Egypt, and other sectors of the Middle East. In the following century red-coated ware became highly popular in Gaul (now France and Belgium). That region continued as the main focus of ceramic production until the 200s A.D., when the pottery-making industries in Roman Britain, Spain, and North Africa overshadowed it.

One of the most exquisite surviving artworks from the potters in southern Gaul is an elegantly decorated red-coated bowl, also in the British Museum collection. In such perfect condition that it looks like it was made last week, it features several delicate ornamented bands that rise from the base. The middle band has wonderfully conceived impressions of flowers and buds attached to long stems that seem to flow like gentle waves. These effects, the museum scholar says, were "achieved through impressing the designs onto the interior of a [wooden] mold, and the vessel was then thrown in the mold, which was mounted on a potter's wheel. This production technique allowed vessels to be produced uniformly in large numbers, usually by workshops in which ten to fifteen potters worked simultaneously."[58]

Artistry in Metal

Ceramics was not the only ancient craft that employed molds to cast objects. Another was metalworking, which explains in part why potters sometimes imitated stylistic elements common in metalwork (as in the Arretine jug in the British Museum). Like the Greeks and other ancient peoples, the Romans used various metals for a wide range of products. These included tools, weapons, armor, coins, statues, jewelry, cooking pots, and wine goblets, among many others. In most of these categories, the finest examples have come to be viewed as art.

The Romans exploited several metals, some in their pure form and others in the form of alloys, or mixtures, of separate metals. The metals included copper, tin, iron, lead, gold, silver, bronze (copper plus tin), brass (copper plus zinc), pewter (lead plus tin), and electrum (gold plus silver). Each metal initially came from an ore, a rock containing veins or pockets of the metal, so it was necessary to separate the two. This was accomplished, often at or near the mine from which the ore had come,

This bronze first-century-B.C. sculpture was found at Herculaneum. Exquisite detail and additions of glass eyes and precious metals were a common Roman practice.

by placing the ore in an extremely hot charcoal-burning furnace. The heat melted down and separated out the metal portion. Workers then poured the softened metal into prepared molds. The result was square- or rectangular-shaped metal ingots, which were delivered to the individual metalworkers or manufacturing centers that had ordered them.

Of these ingots, the ones containing bronze were by far the most common in the Greco-Roman world. This was because bronze was used for more individual items than any other metal. To create those items, metalworkers employed several effective casting methods borrowed from the Greeks. Archaeologist Roy A. Adkins describes them:

> Objects could be made by being cast in stone molds or by the lost wax method. [In the latter] a beeswax model [of the desired item] was covered in clay and fired, melting the wax. Molten bronze was poured into the hollow [area], and when [it] solidified, the clay was removed. Larger hollow objects were made by core casting (or hollow casting). One method was to make a rough shape in clay with a wax model around it. This was covered with clay, and bronze pins were inserted so that the clay core remained in place after the wax was melted in the firing. Molten bronze was poured into the gap left by the wax. The outer clay mold was removed . . . [and then] the clay core was removed through a hole, which was sealed over with bronze.[59]

The largest and often the most stunning Roman bronze artworks were life-size or larger-than-life-size statues of people and animals, made by the hollow-casting process. Usually the torso, head, and limbs were cast separately and then joined together. Then the finishing touches were added. According to scholars Colette and Sean Hemingway: "Decorative details such as hair and other surface design [were] emphasized by means of cold working with a chisel. The ancient Greeks and Romans frequently added eyes inset with glass or stones; teeth and fingernails inlaid with silver; and lips and nipples inlaid with copper, all of which contributed to a bronze statue's as-tonishingly lifelike appearance."[60]

Some of the finest of all Roman metal artworks were gold and silver jewelry and plate (a general term referring to objects made from sheets of metal, especial silver and gold). For jewelry, artisans cut very thin sheets of gold or silver into narrow strips or even wires. Pieces of these strips and wires were then manipulated to form earrings of various shapes, small chain links for necklaces, and so forth. To make a fine dinner dish or serving tray, an artisan carefully hammered a gold or silver sheet into a shallow mold and polished away the hammer marks. He then carved details into the soft metal. One of the supreme masterpieces of Roman silverwork is the so-called Great Dish, made in Roman Britain in the fourth century B.C. It depicts a complex scene in which sea nymphs ride various sea creatures and the fertility god Bacchus parties with his worshippers.

Coin Portraits

Another way the Romans created art from metal was in the production of coins. Like most people today, they viewed coins partly as practical objects, namely as tokens with which to buy things. Yet they also saw them as a type of portrait sculpture that captured the likenesses of national leaders in an age in which photography did not exist and many people otherwise had no idea what those leaders looked like. In Michael Grant's words: "Coins were more portable than busts, and more widely distributed. So, for the [distribution] of the ruler's features, the fullest possible use was made of the coinage. Coin portraits had their share of the [reverence] accorded to imperial statues, for the coinage was itself under divine patronage, and was, in due course, even described as 'sacred.'"[61]

Because coins bearing the emperor's image were seen as a type of portraiture, as well as an artifact blessed by the gods, they also fell into the category of art. Scholar C.H.V. Suther-land writes:

Viewed simply as a sequence of artistic creation, the coinage of the Western world presents a fine and consistent continuity, combined with a [high rate of] survival, which perhaps no other art-form could surpass. . . . At nearly all times, coins have shown directness of appeal, essential humanity, and a quality [that] rises above the merely simple. For the art expressed in coinage is a preeminently social art. . . . They have in most periods reflected the spirit of their time.[62]

Some individual Roman coins can be considered art simply for their masterfully carved miniature faces. Others are also valuable as parts of larger sets or series of coins issued by the

The Romans used coins as "portable busts" to widely distribute likenesses of emperors. Here, the obverse side of a denarius shows the head of the emperor Claudius, while his wife Agrippina, appears on the opposite side .

government. Perhaps the most priceless example was the series of coins put out by the emperor Hadrian (reigned A.D. 117–138), who traveled extensively throughout the realm. "On an unparalleled series of coins," Grant remarks, "he commemorated his own visits to no less than eighteen provinces or territories."[63] The front of each coin in the set bore the ruler's likeness, and the back featured a beautifully carved scene unique to the particular region he had visited.

Roman Glass

Still another Roman craft that produced a number of artistic masterpieces was glasswork. Roman glassmakers borrowed most of their techniques from the extensive glassmaking industry

that developed in the first millennium B.C. in northern Syria. As Rosemarie Trentinella says: "The Roman glass industry owed a great deal to eastern Mediterranean glassmakers, who first developed the skills and techniques that made glass so popular that it can be found on every archaeological site, not only throughout the Roman Empire but also in lands far beyond its frontiers."[64]

The three principal Roman glassmaking centers during the late Republic were Rome, Puteoli (on the Bay of Naples), and Aquileia (in northern Italy). Later, in the early Empire, most of Rome's major provinces developed glassmaking industries, too. Glass objects were initially quite costly, in part because the

This first-century-A.D. glassware came from Aquileia, one of Rome's main glass-making centers in northern Italy.

THE MOLD-BLOWING TECHNIQUE

After the introduction of glassblowing in the first century B.C., *some creative glassmakers found a way to combine glass-casting and pottery-molding methods with the new glassblowing process. The result was a new technique called mold blowing, explained here by a leading expert:*

A craftsman created a mold of a durable material, usually baked clay and sometimes wood or metal. The mold comprised at least two parts, so that it could be opened and the finished product inside removed safely. . . . Next, the glassblower—who may not have been the same person as the mold maker—would blow a gob of hot glass into the mold and inflate it to adopt the shape and pattern carved therein. He would then remove the vessel from the mold and continue to work the glass while still hot and malleable, forming the rim and adding handles when necessary. Meanwhile, the mold could be reassembled for reuse.

Rosemarie Trentinella. "Roman Mold-Blown Glass." New York Metropolitan Museum of Art. www.metmuseum .org/toah/hd/rmold/hd_rmold.htm.

production methods were difficult and time-consuming. Probably the most common technique was to cover a mud or clay core with hot, liquid glass and allow the latter to cool. The artisan then painstakingly removed the core material. A perfect shape and consistent thickness were hard to attain using this approach.

This situation changed significantly in the early years of the Empire, however. In the first century B.C., someone in the Syrian glass industry invented glassblowing, which allowed artisans to make bottles, jars, perfume flasks, and other glass items quicker, cheaper, and with more precision. According to one modern expert:

The new technology revolutionized the Italian glass industry, stimulating an enormous increase in the range of shapes and designs that glassworkers could produce. A glassworker's creativity was no longer bound by the technical restrictions of the laborious casting process, as blowing allowed for previously unparalleled versatility and speed of manufacture. These advantages spurred a rapid evolution of style and form, and experimentation with the new technique led craftsmen to create novel and unique shapes. Examples exist of flasks and bottles shaped like foot sandals, wine barrels, fruits, and even helmets and animals.[65]

Glass breaks and shatters easily, of course, so only a few examples of Roman glasswork have survived in mint condition. As might be expected, many of these come from undisturbed graves and tombs, where the glass items were protected over

This exquisitely carved glass cameo of the *Toilet of Venus* attests to the Romans' superb craftsmanship in the art of glass making.

the centuries. An outstanding example is a beaker made of an attractive light greenish-blue glass found in a first-century-B.C. grave from Roman Britain. Like the red-coated bowl from Gaul, it looks like someone made it only recently. Along with a number of surviving Roman buildings, bridges, roads, sculptures, and mosaics, these splendid items are remnants of the timeless arts produced by one of the most ambitious, industrious, and accomplished peoples ever to walk the earth.

Notes

Introduction: Practical Means for Practical Ends

1. Edith Hamilton. *The Roman Way*. New York: Norton, 1993, p. 155.
2. Hamilton. *The Roman Way*, pp. 156–157.
3. Mortimer Wheeler. *Roman Art and Architecture*. New York: Thames and Hudson, 1994, p. 9.
4. Michael Grant. *Art in the Roman Empire*. London: Routledge, 1995, p. xviii.

Chapter 1: Greeks, Etruscans, and Romans

5. Sallust. *The War with Catiline*. Translated by John C. Rolfe. Cambridge, MA: Harvard University Press, 1931, p. 99.
6. Naphtali Lewis. *Life in Egypt Under Roman Rule*. Oxford: Clarendon, 1999, p. 10.
7. Grant. *Art in the Roman Empire*, p. xvii.
8. Wheeler. *Roman Art and Architecture*, p. 9.
9. Nancy H. Ramage. *Roman Art*. New York: Prentice Hall, 2008, p. 33.

10. Graeme Barker and Tom Rasmussen. *The Etruscans*. Malden, MA: Blackwell, 2000, p. 4.
11. Arthur E.R. Boak and William G. Sinnigen. *A History of Rome to 565 A.D.* New York: Macmillan, 1977, pp. 33–34.
12. Paul Zanker. *Roman Art*. Los Angeles: J. Paul Getty Museum, 2010, pp. 2–3.
13. Fred S. Kleiner. *A History of Roman Art*. Belmont, CA: Wadsworth, 2010, p. 1.

Chapter 2: Amphitheaters and Other Giant Structures

14. Hamilton. *The Roman Way*, p. 155.
15. Leonardo B. Dal Maso. *Rome of the Caesars*. Translated by Michael Hollingworth. Rome: Bonechi-Edizioni, no date, p. 8.
16. Quoted in Peter Quennell. *The Colosseum*. New York: Newsweek Book Division, 1981, p. 89.
17. Tacitus. *The Annals of Ancient Rome*. Translated by Michael Grant. New York: Penguin, 1989, p. 188.
18. Quoted in Jo-Ann Shelton, ed. *As The Romans Did: A Sourcebook in*

Roman Social History. New York: Oxford University Press, 1998, p. 344.

19. D.S. Robertson. *A Handbook of Greek and Roman Architecture*. London: Cambridge University Press, 1980, pp. 285–286.
20. Vitruvius. *On Architecture*. Vol. 2. Translated by Frank Granger. Cambridge, MA: Harvard University Press, 2002, p. 285.
21. Lesley Adkins and Roy A. Adkins. *Handbook to Life in Ancient Rome*. New York: Facts On File, 2004, p. 141.
22. Adkins and Adkins. *Handbook to Life in Ancient Rome*, p. 140.
23. Quoted in Elaine Fantham et al. *Women in the Classical World*. New York: Oxford University Press, 1994, p. 334.
24. Matthew Bunson. *A Dictionary of the Roman Empire*. New York: Oxford University Press, 1995, p. 51.
25. Grant. *Art in the Roman Empire*, p. 72.

Chapter 3: Aqueducts, Water Systems, and Bridges

26. Pliny the Elder. *Natural History*. In *Pliny the Elder: Natural History: A Selection*, translated by John H. Healy. New York: Penguin, 1991, p. 358.
27. Sextus Julius Frontinus. *The Aqueducts of Rome*. In *The Stratagems and the Aqueducts of Rome*, trans-

lated by C.E. Bennett. Cambridge, MA: Harvard University Press, 1993, pp. 357–359.
28. L.A. Hamey and J.A. Hamey. *The Roman Engineers*. Cambridge: Cambridge University Press, 1981, p. 9.
29. Vitruvius. *On Architecture*, p. 189.
30. Vitruvius. *On Architecture*, p. 187.
31. Frontinus. *The Aqueducts of Rome*, pp. 433–437.
32. Frontinus. *The Aqueducts of Rome*, pp. 399, 405.
33. Colin O'Connor. *Roman Bridges*. Cambridge: Cambridge University Press, 1993, p. 188.

Chapter 4: Roads, the "True Art of Rome"

34. Hamilton. *The Roman Way*, p. 157.
35. Lionel Casson. *Travel in the Ancient World*. Baltimore: Johns Hopkins University Press, 1994, p. 163.
36. Procopius. *The Gothic War*. Translated by H.B. Dewing. Project Gutenberg. www.gutenberg.org/files/20298/20298-h/20298-h.htm#Footnote_68_68.
37. Casson. *Travel in the Ancient World*, p. 170.
38. Procopius. *The Gothic War*.
39. Hamey and Hamey. *The Roman Engineers*, p. 22.
40. Raymond Chevallier. *Roman Roads*. London: Batsford, 1989, pp. 116–117.
41. Quoted in Casson. *Travel in the Ancient World*, p. 206.

42. Quoted in Jennifer Viegas. "Ancient Roman Rest Stop Discovered." Discovery Channel. http://dsc.discovery.com/news/briefs/20041129/romanreststop.html.

43. F.R. Cowell. *Life in Ancient Rome.* New York: Putnam, 1976, p. 141.

Chapter 5: Painting, Mosaics, and Sculpture

44. Ludwig Friedlander. *Roman Life and Manners in the Early Empire.* Charleston, SC: Nabu, 2010, p. 325.

45. New York Metropolitan Museum of Art. "Roman Painting." www.metmuseum.org/toah/hd/ropt/hd_ropt.htm.

46. Grant. *Art in the Roman Empire*, p. 93.

47. Josephus. *The Jewish War.* Translated by G.A. Williamson. New York: Penguin, 2000, p. 385.

48. Pliny. *Natural History*, pp. 328–329.

49. New York Metropolitan Museum of Art. "The Roman Mosaic from Lod, Israel." www.metmuseum.org/special/se_event.asp?OccurrenceId={6C51E9CC-0958-4743-A2FE-4A3304C3AAD9}.

50. Adkins and Adkins. *Handbook to Life in Ancient Rome*, p. 170.

51. Pliny. *Natural History*, p. 324.

52. Wheeler. *Roman Art and Architecture*, pp. 152–153.

53. Rosemarie Trentinella. *Roman Portrait Sculpture: Republican Through Constantinian.* Metropolitan Museum of Art. www.metmuseum.org/toah/hd/ropo/hd_ropo.htm.

54. Wheeler. *Roman Art and Architecture*, pp. 164–165.

55. Donald R. Dudley. *The Romans: 850 B.C.–A.D. 337.* New York: Barnes and Noble, 1994, p. 146.

Chapter 6: Ceramics, Metalwork, and Other Crafts

56. J.W. Hayes. "Roman Pottery." Novaesium Alias Neuss. www.novaesium.de/artikel/keramik.htm.

57. British Museum. "Sigillata Jug, Arretine Ware." www.britishmuseum.org/explore/highlights/highlight_objects/gr/s/sigillata_jug.aspx.

58. British Museum. "Sigillata Jug, Arretine Ware."

59. Adkins and Adkins. *Handbook to Life in Ancient Rome*, p. 332.

60. Colette Hemingway and Sean Hemingway. "The Technique of Bronze Statuary in Ancient Greece." New York Metropolitan Museum of Art. www.metmuseum.org/toah/hd/grbr/hd_grbr.htm.

61. Michael Grant. *Roman History from Coins.* London: Cambridge University Press, 1968, p. 13.

62. C.H.V. Sutherland. *Art in Coinage.* London: Batsford, 1956, pp. 15–16.

63. Grant. *Roman History from Coins*, p. 54.

64. Rosemarie Trentinella. "Roman Glass." New York Metropolitan Museum of Art. www.metmuseum.org/toah/hd/rgls/hd_rgls.htm.

65. Trentinella. "Roman Glass."

Glossary

amphitheater: An oval-shaped structure in which the Romans staged public games and shows, especially gladiatorial bouts.

apse: A semicircular chamber extending from one or both ends of a basilica.

arcade (or viaduct): A continuous row of arches and their supports.

arch: An architectural form, usually shaped like a semicircle, used to span the top of a door, window, bridge support, or other open space.

barrel vault: A long curved ceiling.

basilica: A building with a large, high-ceilinged central space, used for court trials and public meetings.

capital: The top section of an architectural column.

chorobates: A wooden device shaped like a bench, used by Roman surveyors to ensure that the ground or a foundation was level.

cinnabar: Mercury sulfide; a mineral used to make red pigment for paints.

circus: A long wooden or stone structure in which the ancient Romans staged horse and chariot races.

cistern: A reservoir for catching and storing rainwater.

coffer dam: A large, boxlike device with no top or bottom that was lowered into a river and drained of water to allow bridge builders to install the foundations of the piers.

consul: In the Roman Republic, one of two jointly serving chief government administrators, who also commanded the armies.

Corinthian: An architectural order characterized by columns with complex clusters of masonry leaves on the capitals.

cursus publicus: "Government post"; an official courier service set up by the emperor Augustus.

Doric: An architectural order characterized by columns with simple, flat capitals.

euripus (or *spina*): The long, narrow, highly ornamented barrier running down the middle of a Roman racetrack.

forum: A Roman city's main square, used for public gatherings and/or as a marketplace.

fresco: A painting done on wet plaster.

hippodrome: A large, open area used by the Greeks and early Romans to stage horse and chariot races.

imagines: In ancient Rome, realistic death masks of deceased relatives.

Ionic: An architectural order characterized by columns with scroll-shaped volutes on the capitals.

itineraria: "Itineraries"; guidebooks that listed towns, inns, and other stops along the major Roman roads.

keystone: The central, topmost stone in an arch.

masonry: Stone or brick.

miliaria: Milestones set up at intervals of a Roman mile along the major roads.

monumental: Large scale.

munus **(plural** *munera***):** "Offering"; a public show involving gladiators.

nave: The large, open space in the center of a basilica.

order: An architectural style, usually identified by the main features of its columns.

pantheon: "All gods"; the group of gods worshipped by a people or nation.

patricians: Members of Rome's wealthiest and most privileged class.

pediment: A triangular gable at the top of the front or back of a Greco-Roman temple.

pier: A vertical support for an arch or other section of a building.

pilaster: A rectangular, ornamented half column, usually recessed partway into a wall.

pteron: A row of columns extending all the way around a temple or other Greek building.

radial: Projecting outward from the center like the spokes of a wheel.

scaenae frons: In a Roman theater, the wall behind the stage on which scenery was painted or hung.

specus: The water channel constituting the heart of an aqueduct.

terra-cotta: Baked clay.

terra sigillata: Also called Samian ware, or red-coated ware, a reddish-colored pottery produced by Roman artisans.

tesserae: Individual cubes or tiles used to make mosaics.

travertine: A durable, finely textured, creamy-white variety of limestone often employed in Roman construction.

triumphal paintings: In ancient Rome, paintings depicting battles and other war-related subjects.

tufa: A lightweight stone composed of compressed volcanic ash, used extensively in Roman buildings.

vault: An elaboration or extension of an arch into three dimensions; or a curved ceiling.

via: A wide or major road.

volute: A spiral- or scroll-shaped decoration on the capital of an Ionic column.

voussoir: One of several individual wedge-shaped stones that form the curve of an arch.

For More Information

Books

Jean-Pierre Adam. *Roman Building: Materials and Techniques*. Translated by Anthony Mathews. Bloomington: Indiana University Press, 2003. A large, comprehensive, authoritative study of all aspects of Roman building.

Lesley Adkins and Roy A. Adkins. *Handbook to Life in Ancient Rome*. New York: Facts On File, 2004. This easy-to-read compilation of data about ancient Roman society contains general overviews of all the Roman arts, as well as thumbnail sketches of many ancient artists.

Lionel Casson. *Travel in the Ancient World*. Baltimore: Johns Hopkins University Press, 1994. Casson, one of the finest classical scholars of the past century, here provides an entertaining sketch of many aspects of Roman daily life and institutions, including roads and water systems.

Sextus Julius Frontinus. *The Stratagems and the Aqueducts of Rome*. Translated by C.E. Bennett. Cambridge, MA: Harvard University Press, 1993. Water commissioner for the city of Rome in the late first century A.D., Frontinus left behind this priceless collection of facts about the aqueducts supplying the Empire's capital.

Michael Grant. *Art in the Roman Empire*. London: Routledge, 1995. This book by one of the most prolific classical scholars provides brief discussions of Roman portraiture, relief sculptures, architecture, paintings, mosaics, coins, gems, and silver work.

Michael Grant. *Roman History from Coins*. London: Cambridge University Press, 1968. Provides considerably more detail on coinage as a form of artistic portraiture.

L.A. Hamey and J.A. Hamey. *The Roman Engineers*. Cambridge: Cambridge University Press, 1981. A short, very easy-to-read but also informative sketch of Roman building materials and techniques, aided by many black-and-white photos and drawings of Roman construction.

Edith Hamilton. *The Roman Way*. New York: Norton, 1993. A famous classical scholar waxes poetic about the Romans—their character, thinking, faults, strengths, and achievements, including their arts.

111

Anthony Marks and Graham Tingay. *The Romans*. London: Usborne, 2003. Aimed at middle-grade and younger readers, this is an overview of Roman history, life, and arts; includes numerous beautiful illustrations.

Colin O'Connor. *Roman Bridges*. Cambridge: Cambridge University Press, 1993. The definitive modern source on Roman bridges, written by a noted bridge engineer who is also an excellent historian; contains long, detailed sections on Roman roads, aqueducts, and the bridges that adorned them, along with appropriate photos.

Pliny the Elder. *Natural History*. In *Pliny the Elder: Natural History: A Selection*, translated by John H. Healy. New York: Penguin, 1991. Pliny's enormous compendium of facts about his world includes many descriptions of Greek and Roman arts.

Peter Quennell. *The Colosseum*. New York: Newsweek Book Division, 1981. A general overview of all aspects of the Colosseum, one of the greatest of Rome's artistic achievements.

Nancy H. Ramage. *Roman Art*. New York: Prentice Hall, 2008. This very readable volume is viewed by many scholars as the best general recent study of a wide range of Roman arts.

Andrew Wallace-Hadrill. *Houses and Society in Pompeii and Herculaneum*. Princeton, NJ: Princeton University Press, 1996. One of the better books about the famous buried Roman cities; contains numerous photos of wall paintings found in the ruins.

Mortimer Wheeler. *Roman Art and Architecture*. New York: Thames and Hudson, 1994. Wheeler, formerly the administrator of the London Museum, wrote this comprehensive study that includes many color photographs and illustrations.

Paul Zanker. *Roman Art*. Los Angeles: J. Paul Getty Museum, 2010. One of the foremost historians of Roman art here delivers an excellent general overview of the subject in straightforward, easy-to-read prose.

Websites

The Alexander Mosaic, Kapteyn Institute (www.astro.rug.nl/~weygaert/alexandermosaic.html). A thorough presentation of the famous Roman mosaic found in Pompeii and thought to be based on an earlier Greek painting.

Ancient Roman Architecture, Great Buildings Online (www.greatbuildings.com/types/styles/roman.html). This site presents a very useful list of links to articles about famous Roman structures, including the Arch of Constantine, Hadrian's Villa, and the House of the Faun in Pompeii.

The Circuses: Roman Chariot Racing, Barbara F. McManus, College of New Rochelle (www.vroma.org/~bmcmanus/circus.html). This is a well-written general overview of Roman chariot racing.

A Day at the Baths, PBS *Secrets of Lost Empires* (www.pbs.org/wgbh/ nova/lostempires/roman/day.html). A virtual tour of a large Roman bathhouse, including recent photos of excavated sections of these structures.

The Pantheon, Great Buildings Online (www.greatbuildings.com/build ings/Pantheon.html). The Pantheon, which still stands in almost perfect condition in Rome, is described here in considerable detail, along with many beautiful photos of it.

The Peutinger Map, Livius Articles on Ancient History (www.livius.org pen-pg/peutinger/map.html). An excellent article on the famous Roman map showing the Empire's main highways.

Pliny the Elder, Livius Articles on Ancient History (www.livius.org/ pi-pm/pliny/pliny_e.html). This informational piece tells about the great Roman naturalist who wrote about Greek and Roman arts.

The Roman Colosseum, Great Buildings Online (www.greatbuildings .com/buildings/Roman_Colosseum. html). A site about the great structure where many Roman spectacles took place. It features color pictures and a list of sources for further reading.

Index

House of the Vettii (Pompeii), 79

I
Inns/lodging houses, 69–71
  thermopilium in, *72*
Ionic columns, 25

J
Jewelry, 99
Josephus (Jewish historian), 81–82
Juno (deity), 22
Jupiter (deity), 22

K
Keystone, 36
Kleiner, Fred S., 26

L
Later Empire (284–476 A.D.), 17
Lewis, Naphtali, 16
Livy (historian), 68
Lost Ram (painting), 80–81
Lucian of Samosata, 44

M
Metalworking, 96, 98–99
Milestones, 66
Minerva (deity), 22
Mold blowing, 103
Monarchy era (753–509 B.C.), 14
  road building in, 61

Mosaic(s), 82–85, *83*
  floor (Israel), *84*
Mount Vesuvius, 32
Munera (fights), 31

N
Natural History (Pliny the Elder), 80
Nerva (emperor), 53, *86*

O
Octavian (emperor), 16–17
On Architecture (Pollio), 41

P
Paintings
  of Pompeii city scene, *77*
  techniques/pigments used in, 76, 78
  themes of, 81–82
Persian Empire, 61
Pliny the Elder, 46, 80, 82
Pollio, Marcus Vitruvius, 41
Polybius (Greek historian), 26
Pompeii
  amphitheater in, 32–33, *33*
  destruction of, 32
  mosaic depicting battle of Issus at, *83*
  wall murals of, 78–81, *79*
Pons Sublicius (bridge), 56
Pont du Gard (France), *49*, 58–59
Portrait busts, 11, *15*, 85, *86*
  recycling of, 86

W
Water, testing purity of, 50
Water distribution system, 51–53, *52*
   fraud in, 53–54

Wheeler, Mortimer, 10, 19, 89

Z
Zanker, Paul, 26

Picture Credits

About the Author

Historian Don Nardo is best known for his books for young people about the ancient and medieval worlds. These include volumes on the arts of ancient cultures, including Mesopotamian arts and literature, Egyptian sculpture and monuments, Greek temples, Roman amphitheaters, medieval castles, and general histories of sculpture, painting, and architecture through the ages. Nardo lives with his wife, Christine, in Massachusetts.